connect

a 9-week small group collision

Living the Faith

Standard PUBLISHING

Cincinnati, Ohio

CD-ROM with printable
student pages enclosed

connect

Published by Standard Publishing, Cincinnati, Ohio
www.standardpub.com

Also available:
Redefining the Win for Jr. High Small Groups, ISBN 978-0-7847-2320-3, copyright © 2010 by CHRIST IN YOUTH
Speak, ISBN 978-0-7847-2406-4, copyright © 2010 by CHRIST IN YOUTH

Printed in: United States of America
Project editor: Kelly Carr
Cover and interior design: Thinkpen Design, Inc., www.thinkpendesign.com

ISBN 978-0-7847-2405-7

15 14 13 12 11 10   1 2 3 4 5 6 7 8 9

Collision Contents

Your Real Goal

by Johnny Scott

We all want to see life change in teens. Many jr. high youth ministries have discovered the importance of assimilating caring adults into the program who value doing life with adolescents. These ministries have also adopted some form of small group meeting time as a part of their larger vision for ministering to jr. highers. Almost everyone agrees that this small group interaction time can be effective. But after being inundated with the vast amount of curriculum and tools for small group leaders, have you ever found yourself back to square one, asking the question of what to do with jr. high small groups?

The answer is in defining what a great small group meeting looks like. In other words, identify the goal and communicate it to the teens in a way that resonates with them.

Without a new way of defining and communicating the wins during every small group session, many leaders feel like they've failed. Teens get frustrated just like we do, and they pick up on our disappointment with small group time. Some leaders have unrealistic expectations of jr. highers. But the fact is that many teens are not capable of articulating what God is doing in their hearts and minds. Many of these small group experiences are seeds that may not be seen for years. We want adolescents to have that breakthrough.

The act of processing faith issues in an environment with caring adults is a pathway we want to familiarize teens with. This in itself is a major win for a small group. Jr. highers are like wet cement. Very quickly they will be set in their ways. How awesome it is when teens begin to process their thoughts about faith and life in the context of a church small group! That's the payoff, and it can happen!

Constantly redefine the win! Question what you do now, and don't be afraid to experiment with redefining your jr. high small group wins. Here are some win-defining ideas from what others are doing:

- Define the win as one kid finally accepting the hug you have been offering for months.
- Define the win as kids not wanting to leave as soon as the official time is over.
- Define the win as someone remembering *anything* from last week.
- Define the win as pairing caring adults with teens.
- Define the win as trusting the Holy Spirit that more is getting through than meets the eye.
- Define the win as jr. highers simply coming back for more.
- Define the win as knowing adolescents feel loved and not manipulated.
- Define the win as adults being determined to look teens in the eye and simply listen as long as they need to talk. (If you did this at small group, it was a huge win!)
- Define the win as anything that shows you are building a relational bridge with a jr. higher!

Has a kid told you about an event happening in his life this week? It wasn't just conversation. Read between the lines. Are your teens anxious, do they want you to attend their events but don't know how to ask?

Unless they are being forced to attend small group by their parents, jr. highers do have other options. If they decided to come on their own to small group, that's a win.

Did a parent help bring them? That is a win because they feel strongly enough about their involvement to invest the time, gas, and hassle of dropping their teens off and picking them up. That is a huge win you needn't overlook. Did you get the chance to connect with that parent and say thanks? That is a bridge.

Did you get to appropriately touch every kid and say something below the surface level about who they are in God's eyes? If that is *all* you did, the whole evening was a hit! That doesn't happen at school and maybe not even at home.

Did someone bring a friend? That is a big deal if they trust you enough to let you in on their world with their friends.

Did someone express any thought that occurred to them during the week concerning last week's content? That is a huge win, and you must celebrate it. Encourage and praise any teen's attempt to take their faith into other parts of their lives. 🌟

For more great strategies, tips, and encouragement,
check out Johnny Scott's *Redefining the Win for Jr. High Small Groups*,
available from Standard Publishing (ISBN 978-0-7847-2320-3).

Before You Begin

Set list

We've broken each session of this Small Group Collision into sections that can be easily taken apart or rearranged so that you only use the elements and the order that works for your kids and their attention span, maturity, etc.

Collision elements

* **txt a frnd**—teens respond to an icebreaker question by texting each other
* **mic check**—teens play a game or do an activity based on the study's theme
* **solo**—teens read and reflect on Scripture for five minutes to prep for the study instead of doing homework before they arrive
* **freestyle**—teens share their reaction to the Scripture or topic by talking or texting
* **strike a chord**—teens study key Scriptures as a group and get into deeper discussion
* **encore**—leader emphasizes key points of the study
* **backstage pass**—teens communicate directly with God through worship, prayer, or contemplation
* **hit the road**—leader wraps up with a focus on life application
* **5 for 5 world tour**—5-minute challenges that teens will do for 5 days each week to put into action what you studied in small group; the leader can send these challenges via text message/e-mail/Facebook/Twitter or print the challenges as a handout from the CD-ROM and send it home with kids

Additional info for the leader

* **hidden track**—helpful tips for the leader about specific activities
* **b4 u meet**—a reminder to send teens before the small group meeting time
* **txt it**—an option in several places during the session allowing teens to text their answers to discussion questions instead of only responding out loud
* **playlist**—songs you may choose to use during your session to relate to the theme
* **aftr u meet**—an encouragement note to send teens after the small group meeting time

Using technology in your small group collision

Text time in the session

Jr. highers love texting. But we don't want them to become distracted by it. So we've come up with a few places in each session where you can allow teens to pull out their cell phones and text the answers to discussion questions to you or to their friends there in small group. Then you can ask them to put their phones away for the remainder of the time. These options allow teens to speak in their communication style within the framework of the small group structure without driving you crazy, we hope! You may choose to use this each session or on occasion.

Music to set the mood

Each session has a playlist of songs that focus on the theme of the study. You may want to download one or more of the songs (or use others you like) to play before, after, or during specific portions of the small group session.

Facebook, Twitter, MySpace

You might want to create your own group on Facebook or start your own Twitter following where all of your jr. highers can join and discuss small group topics during the week. Here you can send reminders to your students about upcoming sessions and post the **5 for 5 world tour** items (see description on previous page). You could also send these via MySpace, text message, or old school e-mail! :)

1

Trading Power and Privilege for Purpose

The Prep

Session goal: Jr. highers will be inspired by Moses' willing sacrifice of power and privilege to live purposefully for Christ, no matter the cost.

Scriptures: Exodus 2; Luke 9:23-25; Luke 14:25-33; Hebrews 11:24-27; Hebrews 12:1, 2

You'll need:

* Bibles
* Pens and pencils
* Paper
* 2 pieces of poster board
* 1 large piece of roll paper
* Tape or something to hang poster and paper
* Colored markers
* 1 garbage can

Download and print:

* "Cloud of Witnesses" handout (1 copy, cut apart)
* **solo/strike a chord** discussion guide (1 per teen)

Optional supplies:

* For **mic check** (option 1): brown paper lunch bags (1 per participant, including any adult leaders and yourself) and a variety of prepackaged snacks, such as miniature candy bars, wrapped candies, cans of soft drinks, small bags of chips, and so on, to go in the bags (several snacks will go in each bag).
* For **backstage pass**: CD player and CD or iPod with recommended **playlist** songs.
* For **hit the road**: Download and print copies of this week's **5 for 5 world tour** take-home page (1 per kid) if you are unable to use the technology options.

Setting it up:

* If you're doing the **mic check** (option 1) activity, divide up the snacks into the paper lunch bags in a variety of combinations. For example, one bag may just have a soft drink can and a caramel, another bag may have 5 different pieces of candy, and another may have some chips and a miniature chocolate bar. You'll need 1 bag of snacks per student.
* Write "He is no fool who gives what he cannot keep . . ." on 1 piece of poster board and hang it on a wall in your meeting room. Set a garbage can directly beneath that poster.
* On the opposite wall in your meeting area, hang the large sheet of roll paper where kids will be able to reach it to write on it. Take the other piece of poster board and write on it: ". . . to gain what he cannot lose" (Jim Elliot). Hang that poster directly above the roll paper. Place markers nearby.

✦ If you'd like to use the optional **playlist** recommendations, download the songs "Keep Quiet" by BarlowGirl, "All I Need" by Bethany Dillon, and "We Won't Be Quiet" by the David Crowder Band and ready your iPod or burn a CD in order to play the songs during the session.

Leader insight:

In Exodus 2:11-15, Moses' decision to leave Egypt doesn't seem very faith-filled. After all, he's just committed murder. In fact, this Scripture paints the picture of Moses fleeing in fear and confusion, hiding away from Pharaoh, who wants him dead. It's not really Moses the faith-hero—it's Moses the cowering criminal.

But while he fled in fear as a murderer, Moses returned from his time in Midian to give up his position of power in Egypt and identify himself with God's people. What happened during his time as a shepherd? Perhaps Moses spent his years sorting out a difficult choice. Should he stay in his life of comfort and power, holding on to his privileged position? Or should he give it all up and throw in his lot with a suffering slave-nation?

It's critical that we step inside the story at this point. There's no skipping ahead here to the burning bush, the plagues, or the parting of the Red Sea. There's no Mount Sinai experience yet, complete with glowing face. Here—right here—it's just Moses and God. It's Moses wrestling with the choice set before him. And when he does make the decision to trade away his privilege for God's sake, as far as he knows, he's simply chosen a life of suffering, shame, and sorrow. But he's willing to do it because he counts suffering alongside God's people a privilege.

What about you? When has God called you to give up something for him? Maybe it was a prestigious job or a good paycheck. Maybe it was your reputation. Maybe you knew you were being misunderstood or judged or mocked. Maybe you've lost friends, or maybe family relationships have suffered. Or maybe it's been little things, like giving up your plans for a day or giving up a TV show you're addicted to. Just as he called Moses to trade away his comfort, he's calling your kids—and he's calling you—to count the cost and make the trade . . . to be willing to give it all for the sake of Christ.

In preparation for leading this small group session, pray: Lord Jesus, thank you for the compelling example of Moses, who counted suffering for your sake a privilege worth far more than riches and power. Teach me, Lord, to keep my sights on you. Help me, Lord, to live with an open hand, willing to give up anything you call me to surrender. And use me, Lord, as I challenge my small group to do the same. Amen.

b4 u meet

A couple of days before your group meets, send a text message to your kids, letting them know how excited you are to begin this Connect study with them. In your text, invite them to start thinking about what kind of connection they have with God right now and what kind of connection they'd like to have with God. (If some kids don't text, send them an e-mail or a message on Facebook or MySpace.)

The Session

Rearrange or delete sections of the study to best meet your group's needs.

txt a frnd   about 5 minutes

Invite your small group to consider this question:
✱ If you had your choice, would you rather be the richest person in the world, the most politically powerful person in the world, the smartest person in the world, or the most athletically talented person in the world? Why?

When they've got an answer, invite them to get out their cell phones and text their answer to another person in the room. (If teens don't have their own phone, they could borrow a friend's or form pairs and talk about their answer to this question.)

When you're ready to move on to the next part of the study, have your kids put their cell phones away for now. ✱

mic check (option 1)   about 7 minutes

Give each teen and adult leader (including yourself) a lunch bag filled with snacks. Invite them to open their bags and look at the contents, but make sure they don't eat anything yet. Encourage them also to look around and see what others have.

Explain the game:
✱ Each person's goal is to end up with the snacks they most want.

* Kids should try to get the snacks they want by mingling with each other and trading snacks. They can make any type of trade they want, such as 1 soft drink can for 3 pieces of candy or 2 miniature chocolate bars for a bag of chips. The only thing they cannot do is trade identical items (such as a Mountain Dew for a Mountain Dew).

hidden track

There are 2 **mic check** options for you. Pick the activity that best fits your group.

* Everyone must make a minimum of 3 trades with 3 different people.
* They've got just 3 minutes to get their ideal snacks.

Answer any questions, then have your jr. highers start trading. Be sure to join in with them in this activity. When time's up, let them start eating the snacks; as they do, invite them to share their reactions to this activity, using questions like these:

* What was it like to trade away your snacks?
* Did you end up with what you wanted in the end? Why or why not?

mic check (option 2) about 7 minutes

Intro this activity by talking about the trade-offs people make in life. For example, people trade their time by doing hard work each day for a paycheck at the end of the week. Then they trade that paycheck for groceries or clothing or a place to live. There are lots of less obvious trades in our world, too. Tell the group you'd like to get their opinion about some of these less obvious trade-offs. Have the kids gather in the center of the room and explain that you'll read a statement, then each person should decide if the statement represents a good trade or a bad trade. Point to the side of the room where you've put the garbage can and tell kids they'll move to that wall if their vote is bad trade. If they think it's a good trade, they'll move to the wall covered with roll paper. Make sure they understand that there's no middle ground—they must give their opinion for each statement by moving throughout the room.

When everyone understands the activity, read each of these statements aloud, allowing time for the kids to move around the room after each one.

* Caitlin Snaring, age 14, won the National Geography Bee in 2007, snagging a $25,000 scholarship. To win the competition, she studied geography 60 hours a week. Good trade? Bad trade?

* The Ferrari Enzo is one of the coolest looking cars on the planet. And besides that, it's amazingly fast and high-tech. But the trade off? To own one you'd have to pay $1 million. Good trade? Bad trade?

* Swimmer Michael Phelps won a record 8 gold medals in the 2008 Olympics. But to get so good and stay in shape, he trades his free time to spend 6 days a week in the pool, often training for 5 hours or more a day. Good trade? Bad trade?

* Picture another kid about your age who is super, super smart. He starts to get made fun of because he's so into school. Eventually he decides to stop studying, to stop doing homework, to stop trying in general. He changes his personality, gains some new friends, and stops getting teased. But he fails his classes and upsets his parents in the process. Good trade? Bad trade?

* Now imagine someone who has an opportunity to become really successful—a writer whose first book was turned into a Hollywood movie and could have many more opportunities in the future. But she decides to pursue poverty instead of wealth, eventually creating a shelter for the homeless and living there herself. Good trade? Bad trade?

* Picture a person who often spends 70 hours a week at the office. She excels at work and gets big raises and bonuses each year. But

she hardly spends any time with her family and often feels totally stressed out. Good trade? Bad trade?

✦ Now picture a young man in a culture hostile to Christianity. He's before the court and is given one last opportunity to publicly swear allegiance to his country's ruler and disown his faith in Christ. He refuses to do so. He's imprisoned and then executed. Good trade? Bad trade?

When you're done, have the kids gather back in the center of the room. ✦

solo about 5 minutes

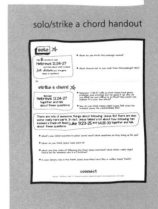

solo/strike a chord handout

Tell your jr. highers you'd like them to find a spot in your meeting area where they can be alone and spend about 5 minutes reading Scripture and thinking about what it means. Explain that Hebrews 11 is a passage in Scripture that is like the Faith Hall of Fame in the Bible, listing various people who lived out their faith in amazing ways. Their job will be to read about just 1 entry in this Hall of Faith: Moses.

Give each teen a copy of the **solo/strike a chord** handout and a pen or pencil, inviting them to read and follow the instructions. (Have them read through only the top portion, **solo**, right now, and they'll need the **strike a chord** portion in a few minutes.) Here's a copy of what they'll read:

Take 5 minutes to read Hebrews 11:24-27. Consider:

✦ What do you think this passage means?

✦ What stands out to you most from this passage? Why?

When the kids understand what they're supposed to do, have them take off and find a spot to read and reflect. After about 5 minutes, call everybody back together. ✦

Cloud of Witnesses handout

hidden track

If you've got less than 8 participants (including yourself), form just 3 groups and discard 1 of the "Cloud of Witnesses" stories. If you've got less than 6 participants, form 2 groups and give each group 2 of the stories to read.

freestyle about 10 minutes

Tell the group that before you talk more about Moses' life, you want them to check out the stories of other real-life people who made similar trades in life. Divide your group into 4 evenly-sized groups (likely pairs or trios). Give each group 1 of the stories from the "Cloud of Witnesses" handout you cut apart before the study.

The groups will be discussing the lives of Vibia Perpetua, Eric Liddell, Dorothy Day, and an anonymous Burmese Christian. Be sure to familiarize yourself with their stories on the "Cloud of Witnesses" handout so you can discuss them further with those who are interested.

Prompt groups to read their assigned story together and share their initial reactions with each other. Then have each group take just 1 minute to explain their story to everybody else, giving them a good picture of that person's life and the trade he or she made.

After all the groups have finished summarizing their stories, lead your group in sharing their reactions to these stories and comparing them to Moses' choice. Use questions like these to guide your discussion:

♦ Which of these 4 stories stands out to you the most? Why?

♦ Do you think these types of stories are common or rare? Why?

♦ How are these stories like or unlike Moses' trade-off?

strike a chord [about 15 minutes]

Provide some info about Moses' background from Exodus 2 for your group. You don't have to read through the entire chapter, but touch on these key points:

♦ When Moses grew up, he was the adopted son of Pharaoh's daughter. He was part of the royal family in one of the most wealthy and powerful nations in all of human history. Egypt was a dominating, formidable power on the world scene, conquering surrounding nations and amassing great riches. Its slave labor force was immense, enabling them to build tremendous palaces and monuments honoring the pharaohs and Egyptian gods. Moses shared in these enormous riches, and he was in line to inherit amazing power.

♦ Moses could've lived a posh, amazing life—a life of power and privilege. He could've had anything he wanted. But Moses made a huge

txt it

You may want to give your teens the option of texting their answers to these questions to you during your discussion time. Read out loud some of their answers and use them as springboards for further discussion. For example, "Kendra texted that the story of the Christian in Myanmar really got to her because it's somebody alive in our world, right now. What do you think when you hear about Christians in our world today having to make such difficult trades?"

solo/strike a chord handout

trade. Because of his faith in God, he chose to suffer mistreatment and misery with God's people rather than enjoy the comforts of life as a prince of Egypt.

✦ But Moses didn't have it all together. He wanted to defend his people, but at first he chose poorly and murdered an Egyptian and fled the country because of it. But while he was away, he had time to think about how fully he would commit to his Hebrew heritage and the one true God. We know in the end that he chose to live the rest of his life devoted to God.

✦ Moses didn't make this trade because he wanted to be a hero that we'd make movies about some day. He didn't do it in order to go down in history. He didn't even do it just to set God's people free. Scripture tells us that he did it "for the sake of Christ" (Hebrews 11:26).

Invite the group to think about Moses' trade: Was it a good trade or a bad trade? Was it worth it for him to trade power, privilege, and wealth to wander in the desert for the rest of his life?

Have the group now look at the bottom portion of the **solo/strike a chord** handout and use it to guide your small group Bible exploration and discussion together as a group. Here's a copy of the **strike a chord** text for you to use to guide your discussion time:

Reread Hebrews 11:24-27 together and discuss these questions:

✦ Hebrews 11:24-27 tells us that Moses had power, privilege, and prestige, but he gave it up. Why do you think he was willing to do that? How would you explain it in your own words?

✦ How do you think Moses might have felt when he traded away his comfortable life?

There are lots of awesome things about following Jesus. But there are also some really hard parts. In fact, Jesus talked a lot about how following him involved a trade-off. Read Luke 9:23-25 and 14:25-33 together and talk about these questions:

✸ What's your initial reaction to Jesus' words here? What questions do they bring up for you?

✸ What do you think Jesus' main point is?

✸ What are the costs of following him that Jesus mentions? What other costs might there be for someone who is a Christian?

✸ In your opinion, how is the faith Jesus describes here like or unlike Moses' faith? ✸

encore   about 5 minutes

Summarize the key ideas your group has shared during your **strike a chord** discussion, then reemphasize the drastic nature of what Jesus said in Luke 9:23, 24 and 14:25-33: Be ready to lose your family; be ready to give up your own hopes and dreams; be ready to even give up your own life!

Challenge your kids with Jesus' words: Like a builder who figures out the costs involved before starting his project, we each need to recognize the costs of following Jesus. As a Christian, there are some things we need to be willing to trade away.

Invite everyone to consider what the price is for us today. What are the costs that we must consider? What might we each individually be asked to give up?

Now lead your group in a short time of prayerful reflection; direct them to close their eyes and silently think about the following questions as you ask them aloud:

✻ What if you faced death or imprisonment for your faith like many Christians around the world do today? Would you still be willing to follow Christ?

✻ What if God called you to share most of your money and possessions with the poor? Would you do it for the sake of Christ?

✻ Or how about something less dramatic. What if following Jesus means you might get made fun of or be misunderstood at school—will you still do it?

✻ What if it means giving up the chance to be liked, to be popular, to be cool?

✻ What if it means speaking about Jesus even if you're nervous or others don't react the way you want?

✻ What if it means giving up a lot of your time? What if God is calling you to quit spending your time on yourself and start spending time caring for others?

✻ What if it means giving up the way you like to talk—giving up gossip or sarcasm or cussing?

✻ What if the cost for you is giving up being selfish or judgmental or angry?

Invite kids to open their eyes, then say something like:
Jesus is calling you to make a trade-off for his sake, just like Moses did. Perhaps God will call you someday to a dramatic choice. But what we're talking about right now are the undramatic choices—choices to boldly live your faith and courageously tell others about it, no matter the cost. ✻

backstage pass `about 8 minutes`

Pass out paper and pens or pencils to all participants. Then read aloud the entire Jim Elliot quote that is posted on your 2 walls. Say something like: What are the things God may be calling you to give up and trade away? Take some time to pray, asking God to challenge you about what he wants you to be willing to give up for his sake.

Explain that when they are ready, they should write down what they are willing to trade away, then walk over to the garbage can, crumple up their paper, and toss it away.

Next, they should cross the room and go to the wall covered with roll paper. There they should use colorful markers to write words or draw symbols, creating a graffiti wall that celebrates the benefits of following Christ.

Encourage participants to have a quiet attitude of prayer during this entire experience. ✦

playlist

To add some powerful ambiance to this prayer experience, download these songs to your iPod (or to a CD) and play them (in this order) while kids pray. Encourage them to listen to the words as well.

"Keep Quiet" by BarlowGirl

"All I Need" by Bethany Dillon"

"We Won't Be Quiet" by the David Crowder Band

hit the road `about 5 minutes`

Have your group gather together and invite a volunteer to read aloud Hebrews 12:1, 2. Then say something like: This should be our response to the story of Moses' faith and to modern-day examples we hear about. These people of faith can inspire us! Their examples can help us and cheer us on as we make the choice to live our entire lives for the sake of Christ.

aftr u meet

Right after your meeting, send kids the first **5 for 5 world tour** challenge for them to do tomorrow via Twitter, e-mail, or by posting it on a Facebook page (or youth group Web page) you've set up. Continue to send 1 challenge each day for the 5 days following your meeting.

About 2 days after your group meets, send a text message to your kids, encouraging them to make a "trade-off" in their life that day. Challenge them to be inspired by Moses' example as they face the pressures of life at school and encourage them to choose Christ, even if it means giving up other things. Prompt them to keep at it with their **5 for 5 world tour** challenges and let them know you're praying for them.

5 for 5 world tour handout

Explain that over the next several weeks you'll dive deeper together into the story of Moses' life and see how it intersects with all of yours. You'll learn together from his successes and failures. You'll discover what his story reveals about the God who desires to connect with each of you. And you'll be inspired to follow Moses' example of faith.

Wrap up with a time of prayer. If they feel comfortable, keep it open for participants to pray aloud. If they're likely to stay silent, lead the prayer yourself, asking God to inspire and strengthen each of the members of your group as they face choices each day to live for Christ.

Let your kids know you'll be sending **5 for 5 world tour** life application and devotional challenges for them to do each day via Twitter, e-mail, or through a Facebook group you've set up. (Or, if you prefer not to use these technology options, pass out copies of the **5 for 5 world tour** handout you've downloaded from the CD-ROM to the teens.) Encourage your kids to strive to spend about 5 minutes each day connecting with God through these devotional experiences.

2

"Who...Me?"

The Prep

Session goal: By exploring Moses' example, jr. highers will learn to view their weaknesses and failings as opportunities to rely on and connect with God.

Scriptures: Exodus 3:1-11; Exodus 3:12; Exodus 4:1-17; 2 Corinthians 12:7-10

You'll need:

* Bibles
* Pens or pencils
* Paper
* Supplies for "Odd-Abilities Olympics" games. The supplies will vary, based on which activities you select. See the list of game ideas in the **mic check** section to determine the supplies you'll need.

Download and print:

* "My Day, My Week, My Year" handout (1 copy per teen)
* **solo/strike a chord** discussion guide (1 per teen)
* "Surrender" handout (1 copy per teen)

Optional supplies:

* For **backstage pass:** CD player and CD or iPod with recommended **playlist** songs.

✦ For **hit the road:** Download and print copies of this week's **5 for 5 world tour** take-home page (1 per teen) if you are unable to use the technology options.

Setting it up:

✦ Read the "Odd-Abilities Olympics" game ideas in **mic check** and select several games your group will do (based on your group size, meeting area, etc.). Collect all needed supplies and set up the challenge stations.

✦ If you'd like to use the optional **playlist** recommendations, download the songs "Olympic Fanfare and Theme" by the Boston Pops Orchestra and "Gonna Fly Now" from the *Rocky* soundtrack and ready your iPod or burn a CD in order to play the songs during the session.

Leader insight:

Unlike later parts of Exodus, the first 4 decades of Moses' life described in Exodus 2 are rather sparse on the details. We learn the story of Moses' birth and then skip ahead to find him as a grown man (Exodus 2:11). We don't know much about his personality, where exactly he lived, or many other details. But as we get to know him better, following him from Egypt through Midian to the burning bush, we start to get the sense that we're seeing 2 different Moseses.

The Moses of Exodus 2:11, 12 is still the prince of Egypt—he is a man of privilege and power, confidence and action. In the face of injustice, he takes matters into his own hands, secretively killing an unjust oppressor. The Moses of Exodus 3, 4, though, appears to have become a man of inaction. He's lived in the wilderness now for years.

And when God calls him to lead the Israelites from Egypt, Moses becomes fixated—frozen almost—on his own fears and weaknesses. "Who . . . me?!" he asks in disbelief. There are many reasons Moses feels unqualified, but one particular roadblock for him is his weakness as a speaker. Exodus 4:10 puts it this way: "O Lord, I'm not very good with words. I never have been, and I'm not now, even though you have spoken to me. I get tongue-tied, and my words get tangled."

But Moses is *right* where God wants him. This is no longer the man who is acting on his own strength and executing his own plans. This is a man who is being forced, in essence, to rely on God every step of the way. In no way will Moses mistake God's power for his own; Moses *knows* the only chance he has on this mission is to trust in the God who made his mouth and who can use it, despite Moses' lack of skill.

Jr. high kids know a lot about insecurity. They fixate on their faults and failings: acne, high-pitched voices, klutziness, being overweight or too skinny, feeling stupid in math, having an inability to look or act cool. Even the most cocky or seemingly confident kids are often using a persona to hide the real fears tucked away inside. This session will meet them right in that area of need—they'll discover that they can turn their weaknesses from sources of fear into avenues of connection with God.

But what about you? You aren't in jr. high anymore—you now have a healthy sense of yourself; you know your skills and talents; you work on your weaknesses. And those are all good things. But do you find yourself relying just a bit too much on your own abilities? Do you trust in your own strength instead of leaning on God? How often do you really seek God's help?

In preparation for leading this small group session, pray:

Lord Jesus, crush overconfidence and self-reliance in my life. Turn my eyes from my own abilities. Wipe out pride and arrogance. Bring me to my knees in a burning-bush awareness that you made me and it is only through your strength and power that I can truly minister to these kids. Thank you for my weaknesses. Help me to live as a vibrant example of God-reliance, not self-reliance. And guide me as I point my kids to the hope they can find in you in the midst of their fears and weaknesses. In Jesus' name, amen.

b4 u meet

A couple of days before your group meets, send a text message to your kids letting them know how excited you are to continue this Connect study with them. (If some teens don't text, send them an e-mail or a message on Facebook or MySpace.)

The Session

Rearrange or delete sections of the study to best meet your group's needs.

txt a frnd `about 5 minutes`

Invite your small group to consider this question:

✳ If you could instantly get a talent or ability that you don't have now, what would you want? Why?

When they've got an answer, invite them to get out their cell phones and text their answer to another person in the room. (If kids don't have their own phone, they could borrow a friend's or could form pairs and talk about their answer to this question.)

When you're ready to move on to the next part of the study, have teens put their cell phones away for now. ✳

mic check `about 15 minutes`

Welcome everyone to the Odd-Abilities Olympics. Explain that your group will break into pairs and work as teams at each game station you've set up. Let them know they can do the challenges in whatever order they'd like. Their goal is to get through as many as possible in the next 10 minutes.

Set up several stations, depending on the size of your group and the space you have. Use our listed games or create your own. Be sure to test a variety of types of skills—mental, physical, and random talents. Here are some ideas:

- **Word Find Challenge:** Set out copies of easy word search puzzles and time how quickly teams can find all the words.
- **Mental Math Challenge:** Have teams solve math problems (addition and subtraction). But don't let them write anything down— they've got to do it all in their heads.
- **Popcorn Catch:** Have teammates stand several feet apart and give 1 a bag of popcorn. One member should toss the popcorn while the other catches it in his or her mouth. Count how many pieces of popcorn are caught and eaten in 60 seconds.
- **Balloon-Volley Challenge:** Have teammates stand several feet apart and bat a balloon back and forth to each other without letting it touch the ground. The tough part? They can't use their hands or arms—they must use legs, feet, knees, heads, shoulders, etc. Count how many times each pair can volley their balloon back and forth.
- **Handstand Challenge:** Time 1 student per pair on how long he or she can hold a handstand.
- **Opera Performance:** Have 1 member per team do an impression of opera by singing the highest note he or she can and holding it as long as possible.
- **Iron Cross Challenge:** Have 1 member per team hold his or her arms straight out to each side, palms up. On each palm should rest 1 thick, hardcover book. Time how long they are able to maintain this position.
- **Stupid Human Tricks:** Have 1 member per team show off an unknown talent they have. For example, they may be able to

playlist

To add to the fun of these games, download these songs to your iPod (or to a CD) and play them while kids compete:
"Olympic Fanfare and Theme" by the Boston Pops Orchestra
"Gonna Fly Now" from the *Rocky* soundtrack

perform a feat of flexibility, roll their tongues, burp the alphabet, hang a spoon off their noses, or do impressions of your church's minister. The sky's the limit!

Explain each station and have them get started. At the end of 10 minutes, have everyone gather back together and discuss:

✱ Which events did you feel skilled enough to do? Which required skills you don't feel you have?

Communicate to your group the fact that we all have skills, but sometimes we look around at other people's skills and we feel that theirs are better while ours are inadequate. But God wants to use our weaknesses as well as our strengths.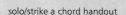

solo `about 5 minutes`

solo/strike a chord handout

Tell your jr. highers you'd like them to find a spot in your meeting area where they can be alone and spend about 5 minutes reading Scripture and thinking about what it means. Remind them that last week they read about Moses' upbringing and how he made the trade-off to leave his royal upbringing and associate with his Hebrew heritage, a people who were slaves. He left Egypt for some years. Now they'll read about the mission God has for him.

Give each teen a copy of the **solo/strike a chord** handout and a pen or pencil, inviting them to read and follow the instructions. (Have them read through only the top portion, **solo**, right now, and they'll need the **strike a chord** portion in a few minutes.) Here's a copy of what they'll read:

Take 5 minutes to read Exodus 3:1-11. Consider:

✽ What stands out to you most from this passage? Why?

✽ Close your eyes and imagine being in God's presence like Moses, on holy ground.

When they understand what they're supposed to do, have them take off and find a spot to read and reflect. After about 5 minutes, call everybody back together. ✽

strike a chord   about 10 minutes

Have the group now look at the bottom portion of the **solo/strike a chord** handout and use it to guide your small group Bible exploration and discussion together as a group. Here's a copy of the **strike a chord** text for you to use to guide your discussion time:

Reread Exodus 3:7-11 together and discuss these questions:

✽ How do you think Moses felt when he was commissioned to lead his people out of Egypt?

✽ Why do you think he responded the way he did in Exodus 3:11?

✽ How would you have felt in his shoes? What would you have said to God?

solo/strike a chord handout

txt it

If you want, invite teens to answer these questions both by talking aloud and by texting. As some share their answers, others can text them to you. Read some of their thoughts aloud and build upon their ideas as your group explores these issues together.

Communicate these ideas to your group:

* God called to Moses out of the burning bush and commissioned him to lead his people out of slavery in Egypt. The most natural question that anyone asks in response to such a call is, "Why me?" Essentially, this is what Moses asks in verse 11.

* Moses is right in one sense. *He* is not the answer to the Israelite's problem. God did not call him because he possessed some extraordinary power apart from God—in fact we'll see soon that Moses lacks skills in a crucial area. But Moses is wrong in another sense. Moses seems to believe in some small way that the call to lead the people out of Egypt is connected to human strength and ability. But there is not any person on the planet that is fully credentialed for this mission.

* God's call is humbling, and this may be the best explanation for Moses' response. In no way can a human soul feel up to a task as great as this. And that is why we would all respond in a similar way as Moses. ⭐

My Day, My Week, My Year handout

My Day, My Week, My Year

1. Rate your **day** by putting an X on the scale below.

1 2 3 4 5 6 7 8 9 10

The worst ever imagined   So-so   Pretty good   100% awesome

2. Rate your **week** by putting an X on the scale below.

1 2 3 4 5 6 7 8 9 10

The worst ever imagined   So-so   Pretty good   100% awesome

3. Rate your **year** by putting an X on the scale below.

1 2 3 4 5 6 7 8 9 10

The worst ever imagined   So-so   Pretty good   100% awesome

connect

txt it

You may want to give your kids the option of texting their ratings and explanations to you during your discussion time. Read some of their answers out loud.

freestyle (part 1)   about 4 minutes

Give each kid a copy of the "My Day, My Week, My Year" handout. Tell them to take a minute and follow the directions by rating their day, their week, and their year. After a minute, have a few people share why they rated their day, week, and year as they did. ⭐

Dig into the message of this study by sharing the following ideas with your group:

✦ For many of us, when we look at our normal life we see nothing special. We consider ourselves disqualified from God's great plans. We see our day, our week, and our year as average, plain, normal, status quo, or even as below-average. And I suspect that this is what Moses did. When he's called to lead his people and he asks "Who am I?" he remembers the shame of committing murder and his fear of Pharaoh's pursuit. He remembers his aimless, nomadic wandering. He remembers his chance meeting with Reuel's daughters and marriage to Zipporah (Exodus 2:11-22).

✦ But if he looked at his life with the right view, he wouldn't see a failed life. Instead he'd see God's guidance through all these incidents. He would see God's providence and his special appointment, culminating in his commission at the burning bush. With this perspective, it all makes sense when Moses hears God's response.

✦ Read aloud Exodus 3:12: "God answered, 'I will be with you. And this is your sign that I am the one who has sent you: When you have brought the people out of Egypt, you will worship God at this very mountain.'"

Say something like: Moses doesn't exactly have high self-esteem at this point in his life. He was too worried about his inabilities. Ever felt this way? Have you ever felt like your faults or weaknesses were just huge, preventing you from being who you want to be in life? Maybe it's something you hate about your appearance. Maybe you feel like a total klutz and you wish you were good at sports—at any sport. Maybe you're struggling with a subject in school and it makes you feel confused or dumb. Maybe you just seem to always say all the wrong things at the wrong times. If you've ever felt this way, then maybe you relate to Moses.

Read Exodus 4:1-17 aloud and invite others to follow along in their Bibles.

Explain to your group that this passage makes it clear to us why God picked Moses. It's like God picked a guy with a big, fat weakness on purpose: So that in no way would Moses be tempted to look to his *own* abilities while leading the people out of Egypt. God would continue to reveal himself through the entire episode. And Moses' one glaring insecurity is in the one place where he'll be required to work for God. God has already called him to speak to the elders of Israel (Exodus 3:16) and Pharaoh (Exodus 3:10) in order to complete his mission, but Moses isn't much of a public speaker!

Reread Exodus 4:10: "But Moses pleaded with the LORD, 'O Lord, I'm not very good with words. I never have been, and I'm not now, even though you have spoken to me. I get tongue-tied, and my words get tangled.'"

Finish up this section by sharing these ideas:

✦ It's possible that Moses had a severe stuttering problem or other speech impediment. Or maybe he just had awful stage fright. We don't know specifically why he's so insecure in this area, but it's obvious that in Moses' mind there must be a better man for the job. But in God's mind, this is exactly why he called Moses.

✦ In the end there would be no mistaking who led the people out of slavery. Accompanied by his staff, a constant reminder of God's call and presence, and numerous signs, Moses' primary qualification appeared to be his weakness. Because of his insecurity, Moses was able to surrender himself to God, the call, and his mission. In this way, he was the perfect man for the job. ✦

freestyle (part 2) `about 5 minutes`

Have kids look at their ratings again on the "My Day, My Week, My Year" handout. Then discuss this question:

✦ In hindsight, how have you seen God at work in your day, your week, or your year? Share a specific example. ✦

backstage pass `about 5 minutes`

Pass out a copy of the "Surrender" handout to each student. You may want them to spread apart a little bit to focus. If you're able, dim the lights in your meeting area.

Instruct kids to read through the prayer 1 time on their own. Then say, We're going to wrap up today with a time for us each to talk to God and surrender ourselves to him. Let's start by quieting our hearts for prayer. Take a moment to quiet your thoughts and focus on God. As random thoughts pop into your head, acknowledge them, and then set them aside to focus on Jesus.

After about 1 minute of silence, read the prayer aloud from the handout:

txt it

You may want to give your teens the option of texting their answers to you. Read some of their answers out loud.

Surrender handout

hidden track

Contrary to popular stereotypes, even hyper-active 7th graders can quiet their hearts before God! This prayer exercise is a great way to introduce your kids to the practice of contemplation. Intentionally incorporating times of silence into your small group collision will help them become more familiar and comfortable with quietness. And the more often they practice it with their friends at youth group, the more likely they'll be to weave it into their everyday lives.

"Take, Lord, and receive all my liberty, my memory, my intellect, and all my will—all that I have and possess.

You gave it to me: to You, Lord, I return it!

All is Yours, dispose of it according to your will.

Give me your love and grace, for this is enough for me."

After a brief pause, but still in the mode of prayer, have them pray about:

✱ What are your skills and abilities? Do you rely too much on yourself, on your own confidence? Right now offer your abilities to God.
Pause at least 1 minute.

✱ What are your fears and insecurities? Offer them to Christ.
Pause at least 1 minute.

✱ What are your inabilities and weaknesses? Surrender them to Jesus for him to use them.

After about 1 more minute, have everyone pray the "Surrender" prayer aloud together. ✱

hit the road `about 1 minute`

Say something like this: Moses felt unqualified and insecure, but that was right where God wanted him. When you face insecurities this week, instead of letting them make you feel bad about yourself, turn things around by connecting with God and relying on him. Put your focus right on him and his power—he will qualify you to answer his call.

Let your kids know you'll be sending **5 for 5 world tour** life application and devotional challenges for them to do each day via Twitter, e-mail, or through a Facebook group you've set up. (Or, if you prefer not to use these technology options, pass out copies of the **5 for 5 world tour** handout you've downloaded from the CD-ROM to the teens.) Encourage your kids to strive to spend about 5 minutes each day connecting with God through these devotional experiences.

aftr u meet

Right after your meeting, send kids the first **5 for 5 world tour** challenge for them to do tomorrow via Twitter, e-mail, or by posting it on a Facebook page (or youth group Web page) you've set up. Continue to send 1 challenge each day for the 5 days following your meeting.

About 2 days after your group meets, send a text message to your kids, encouraging them to keep their weaknesses in perspective and rely on God's strength. Prompt them to keep at it with their 5 for 5 world tour challenges and let them know you're praying for them.

5 for 5 world tour handout

When in Doubt...

The Prep

Session goal:
As they learn about doubt and confusion in the life of Moses, jr. highers will be inspired to keep their eyes on the truths of God.

Scriptures:
Exodus 4:29–5:23; Hebrews 11:1

You'll need:

* Bibles
* Pens or pencils
* Paper
* 9 similarly-sized books
* Pencil or pointer
* 1 large piece of roll paper
* Black markers
* Several sheets of red construction paper
* A few rolls of masking tape

Download and print:

* **solo/strike a chord** discussion guide (1 per teen)
* "Illusion of the Bricks" handout (1 per every 2 teens)
* "My Reality" handout (1 per teen)

Optional supplies:

- For **backstage pass:** CD player and CD or iPod with recommended **playlist** songs.
- For **hit the road:** You may choose to purchase bricks or patio stones (1 per teen). You can get them at your local hardware or garden store for about $0.75 to $1.25 each.
- For **hit the road:** Permanent markers and additional art supplies (paint, brushes, glitter, etc.) to decorate the bricks if you choose to use real bricks.
- For **backstage pass:** Download and print copies of this week's **5 for 5 world tour** take-home page (1 per teen) if you are unable to use the technology options.

Setting it up:

- Recruit one of the teens ahead of time who will be the volunteer during the **mic check** activity. Review how the illusion works with the volunteer and make sure he or she keeps this secret knowledge absolutely confidential.
- Cut the red construction paper into rectangle "bricks" that are approximately 6x9 inches. You'll need 5 rectangles for every pair of teens during the **freestyle** activity. If you are using paper bricks instead of real ones for the **hit the road** section, be sure to cut additional bricks (1 per teen) for this section.
- Prepare the roll paper by writing GOD IS in huge letters. As part of the session, kids will cover these words with their construction paper bricks, so try to estimate the size of your writing accordingly.
- Option: Purchase bricks (or patio stones) for kids to take home at the end of the session. You'll want 1 per teen.

✦ If you'd like to use the optional **playlist** recommendations, download the songs "Falls Apart" by Thousand Foot Krutch, "Fears and Failures" by This Beautiful Republic, and "God Is With Us" by Michael Olson and ready your iPod or burn a CD in order to play the songs during the session.

Leader insight:

Think of the most cringe-worthy moment of your life. Perhaps it was an embarrassing situation or maybe a conversation you bungled by saying the wrong thing. Perhaps it was a time that brought about tears or great regret. Whatever it is, it's that moment you wish you could erase from your life.

OK, now you're ready to step into Moses' shoes at this point in the story. As you studied in the previous session, Moses had serious misgivings about his ability (or lack of) to lead God's people out of Egypt. But now he's accepted the assignment and has come with Aaron to confront Pharaoh. And things go *terribly*. Pharaoh mockingly rejects Moses and Aaron's request. But things get even worse when Pharaoh makes the Hebrews collect their own straw for their bricks—and it's no secret that this injustice is "Moses' fault." Pharaoh's sneaky maneuver succeeds: He turns the Israelites against Moses. They're angry, they reject him as their leader, and they call down God's judgment against him. Not exactly the welcome Moses was hoping for.

And so Moses, in the face of the tremendously discouraging circumstances, does what most of us would do: He doubts God. He's angry, he feels let down, and he's completely questioning his own calling. It's as if God has made a fool of him.

In human terms, Moses has every excuse to be frustrated and confused. The circumstances are truly daunting and discouraging. But in spiritual terms, Moses is way off base. He's let circumstances blind him to the truth of God's presence, God's goodness, and God's sovereign plan. He's taken his eyes off of these spiritual realities and focused on the concrete, present circumstances of his life.

What about you? Does your life, minute by minute, reflect a firm belief in God's constant presence? Or do circumstances, feelings, and challenges easily pull you into doubt or confusion? Or perhaps you don't quite *doubt* God—you just live as if he's not there, acknowledging him during times of need but in other situations your thoughts are focused mostly on the here and now instead of on eternal, spiritual realities. Consider Moses in this moment—before the plagues and the escape through the Red Sea. Consider him here as the very human man that he is—doubts, frustrations, and all—and ask God to solidify *your* faith in the face of challenging situations.

In preparation for leading this small group session, pray: Lord Jesus, open my eyes to your reality and presence in every moment. Rid me of petty doubts. And with the big doubts and tough questions, Lord, help me bring them to you. Help me stay focused on eternal, spiritual realities instead of getting constantly sidetracked by the physical, concrete aspects of life. Help me avoid the "grand illusion"—acting like you aren't even there. And speak through me as I help my kids explore the tough issues of doubt and faith. In Jesus' name, amen.

The Session

Rearrange or delete sections of the study to best meet your group's needs.

b4 u meet

A couple of days before your group meets, send a text message to your kids reminding them of the upcoming Connect study. (If some teens don't text, send them an e-mail or a message on Facebook or MySpace.)

txt a frnd `about 5 minutes`

Invite your group to consider this question:

> ★ Name something you've seen advertised, but you are skeptical that it can do what the ad says it will do. Why did you mistrust this information?

When they've got an answer, invite them to get out their cell phones and text their answer to another person in the room. (If kids don't have their own phone, they could borrow a friend's or could form pairs and talk about their answer to this question.)

When you're ready to move on to the next part of the study, have them put their cell phones away for now. ★

mic check `about 10 minutes`

Invite everyone to gather around you as you set out 9 books on a table in 3 rows of 3. Ask for a volunteer to be your assistant—this should be the volunteer you've made arrangements with before the session began. Then send that volunteer out of the room and explain the game to everyone else.

Show everyone the 9 books and ask the group to choose 1 book. Let the group know that *this* will be the book that the volunteer outside will try to identify.

Invite your assistant back in and tell him that it is his job to correctly guess which book the group picked.

hidden track

If you don't want to do this trick because your kids already know it or might figure it out too easily, try a card trick or some other illusion that you know.

THE SECRET TO THE GAME: Begin by tapping a book with a pencil (or some other type of pointer) and asking, "Is this the one?" This step holds the secret to the game. The assistant should treat the first book you tap as if it were a map—the area that you tap will indicate to him the exact location of the correct book on the table. For example, if you tap the first book in the upper right hand corner, you are indicating that the selected book is the top book in the top row. If you tap in the middle of the first book, the guesser will know that the correct book is the one in the very middle of the 3 rows of 3.

By watching where you've tapped on the first book, the assistant will know which is the correct one. Continue to tap books randomly, asking "Is this the one?" each time. The assistant should answer "yes" or "no" until you've tapped the right book.

Repeat this game with the same volunteer, and then ask other kids if they've figured it out and would like to give it a try.

At the end of the game, ask someone who's figured it out to share the trick with the rest of the group. (If no one has guessed the secret to this trick, have your volunteer explain it.) Thank everyone for playing.

Then say something like this: Did any of you really think that _____ (insert volunteer's name here) had special powers or could read my mind? Why did you doubt? Most magic tricks are just a matter of illusion. Some people think that the idea of God's existence is just an illusion. They have huge questions and doubts, so they think that the only true reality they can trust is what they can see or prove. ✦

solo `about 5 minutes`

T ell your jr. highers you'd like them to find a spot in your meeting area where they can be alone and spend about 5 minutes reading Scripture and thinking about what it means. Remind them that last week they read about Moses' mission from God and how he felt inadequate for the task. Now they're going to look at what happens when the task Moses is supposed to follow doesn't go according to his plan.

solo/strike a chord handout

Give each teen a copy of the **solo/strike a chord** handout and a pen or pencil, inviting them to read and follow the instructions. (Have them read through only the top portion, **solo**, right now, and they'll need the **strike a chord** portion in a few minutes.) Here's a copy of what they'll read:

Take 5 minutes to read Exodus 4:29–5:23. As you read, consider:

✦ What do you think the Israelites were thinking during all of this?

✦ What do you think Moses was thinking?

When they understand what they're supposed to do, have them take off and find a spot to read and reflect. After about 5 minutes, call everybody back together. ✦

strike a chord `about 15 minutes`

S ay something like this: In your Scripture passage, you just read about a time when Moses experienced doubt and confusion. Remind your kids what you've studied the past few sessions and what has happened to Moses up until this point:

solo/strike a chord handout

txt it

If you want, invite kids to answer these questions both by talking aloud and by texting. As some share their answers, others can text them to you. Read some of their thoughts aloud and build upon their ideas as your group explores these issues together.

* Moses left Egypt and lived in the wilderness.
* He met God at the burning bush and was called by God to go on an amazing mission.
* At first Moses was very hesitant, but then he accepted the call. With his brother Aaron at his side, Moses returned to Egypt.
* Moses was ready to confront Pharaoh and rely on God's power to deliver his people from slavery.

Ask a volunteer to summarize what they just read during the **solo** time from Exodus 4:29–5:23. If no one volunteers, summarize the story yourself with something like this:

This isn't exactly the heroic, successful entrance Moses might have dreamed of. This passage is full of failure, discouragement, anger, and doubt.

Pretty quickly after they praised God, the Israelites got really ticked off! They were angry at Moses for good reason: Their awful circumstances just got a whole lot worse!

And Moses' feelings toward God at the end of this passage are also understandable, aren't they? After he went through self-doubt, he finally accepted God's mission and came to confront Pharaoh and free his people. But instead of freeing the slaves, Moses' actions led to even greater injustice against them. And after welcoming Moses as their hero, the Hebrews treated him with anger and contempt.

Have the group now look at the bottom portion of the **solo/ strike a chord** handout, and use it to guide your small group Bible exploration and discussion together as a group. Here's a copy of the **strike a chord** text for you to use to guide your discussion time:

Discuss Exodus 4:29—5:23 together:

✹ How would you have felt if you were a Hebrew slave given the task of making bricks without all the supplies you needed? Why?

✹ Step into Moses' shoes: How would you react after your request to Pharaoh not only got rejected, but it actually made things worse? How would you feel toward God?

✹ Why do you think they let these circumstances get in the way of their trust in God? Would you have felt that way? Why or why not? ✦

freestyle about 15 minutes

Go to your prepared roll paper where you've written GOD IS in large letters. Now ask your kids to brainstorm:

✹ What are some of the important things we believe about God?

Write their answers on the paper surrounding the words GOD IS. (Be sure to edit accordingly if anyone's suggestions are a little off base.) Now say something like, The idea that this world is the only true reality—that God isn't real—is an illusion. People who buy into that are missing out on the truth. And sometimes we buy into the illusion too. Sometimes we doubt or ignore the truths about God. Sometimes we live as if these truths aren't real.

Divide your group into pairs and give each pair a copy of the "Illusion of the Bricks"

Illusion of the Bricks handout

txt it

You may want to give your teens the option of texting their answers to this question.

handout. Also give each pair 5 red bricks you made before the session and markers and tape. Then have them follow the instructions on the page. There are 3 parts to this activity. Make sure each pair has time to finish part 1 before they trade bricks with other groups in part 2. And then have everyone do part 3 at the same time.

hidden track

If you've got only a few participants, you may choose to do this activity as an entire group.

After the group has finished putting the bricks on the GOD IS sign, say something like this: We all experience doubt. We all have moments of weakness in our faith. We lose sight of God and his reality. But we don't have to stay there.

encore   about 3 minutes

Communicate these ideas to your group:
* Like the Hebrews, you may have had times in your life when you were treated totally unfairly. Or a time when you felt singled out or picked on. Or a time when you felt powerless to defend yourself.
* Like Moses, you may have had times when you were trying to do something great for God, like witness to a friend or show kindness to an enemy, and you fell flat on your face. Or maybe the words came out wrong or you chickened out or you got totally misunderstood.

If your group did the **freestyle** activity, point to the wall and say something like this:

We've created a picture of the Grand Illusion. The truth is there—the truth that God is real and he has a plan—but we get blinded by the circumstances in our lives, and we no longer see true reality. All we can see are the concrete realities of our lives, not the spiritual realities. And that's when doubt sneaks up on us and rocks our faith.

Review aloud several of the situations or feelings represented on the brick wall. Then explain to your kids that these things can trip us up and cause us to doubt just as Moses experienced. In Moses' life, this moment was a dark one—he probably felt confused and abandoned. But we don't have to respond to tough circumstances the same way. We can choose, instead, to reject the Grand Illusion and embrace the true reality of the universe. Even when tough circumstances make it hard to see God's reality, we can still choose to believe it and live by it. That's what real faith looks like.

Invite a volunteer to read aloud Hebrews 11:1 while everyone else reads along. Then say something like: This is what real faith looks like. We can't see God, but we know beyond a shadow of a doubt that he's there. We may not understand our circumstances, but we trust that he is in control. We may feel confused, but we still choose to believe that God is good.

backstage pass   about 12 minutes

Give each kid a copy of the "My Reality" handout and a pen. Give them 5 to 8 minutes to prayerfully read through the handout. When time is up,

playlist

To add some upbeat ambiance to this reflection experience, download these songs to your iPod (or to a CD) and play them (in this order) while students work:
"Falls Apart" by Thousand Foot Krutch
"Fears and Failures" by This Beautiful Republic
"God Is With Us" by Michael Olson

My Reality handout

invite everyone to help you tear off the bricks so the GOD IS statement is revealed again. Have everyone throw away all the bricks of doubt. ✦

hit the road

Invite kids to each take a brick (or patio stone) or 1 of the paper bricks you made and use a permanent marker to write GOD IS on their brick. This will be a reminder they can take home to help them stay focused on the reality that should shine through tough circumstances.

5 for 5 world tour handout

Let your kids know you'll be sending **5 for 5 world tour** life application and devotional challenges for them to do each day via Twitter, e-mail, or through a Facebook group you've set up. (Or, if you prefer not to use these technology options, pass out copies of the **5 for 5 world tour** handout you've downloaded from the CD-ROM to the teens.) Encourage your kids to strive to spend about 5 minutes each day connecting with God through these devotional experiences. ✦

hidden track

If you purchased real bricks (or patio stones), you may want to provide additional art supplies kids can use to decorate their bricks.

aftr u meet

Right after your meeting, send your kids the first **5 for 5 world tour** challenge for them to do tomorrow via Twitter, e-mail, or by posting it on a Facebook page (or youth group Web page) you've set up. Continue to send 1 challenge each day for the 5 days following your meeting.

About 2 days after your group meets, send a text message to your kids, encouraging them to keep facing their doubts with the truths of God. Prompt them to keep at it with their **5 for 5 world tour** challenges, and let them know you're praying for them.

Where's Your Focus?

The Prep

Session goal:
Jr. highers will learn, as Moses did, to focus on who God is.

Scriptures:
Exodus 3:13-15; Exodus 5:22–6:23; Psalm 139:1-18

You'll need:

* Bibles
* Pens or pencils
* Paper
* Art supplies (pens, colored pencils, markers, paint, etc.)
* Printouts of optical illusions (see **Setting it up** for details)

Download and print:

* **solo/strike a chord** discussion guide (1 per teen)
* "Misperceptions" handout (1 copy, cut apart)

Optional supplies:

* For **backstage pass:** CD player and CD or iPod with recommended **playlist** songs.
* For **hit the road:** Download and print copies of this week's **5 for 5 world tour** take-home page (1 per teen) if you are unable to use the technology options.

Setting it up:

✦ Look up "optical illusions" online and find several to print out and show your kids during **mic check**.
✦ Cut apart the "Misperceptions" handout into 4 sections.
✦ Have a variety of art supplies available for **backstage pass**.
✦ If you'd like to use the optional **playlist** recommendations, download the songs "Only True God" by Kathryn Scott, "How Great is Our God" by Chris Tomlin, and "We're Amazed" by The Longing and ready your iPod or burn a CD in order to play the songs during the session.

Leader insight:

Why, God?

It often feels like a fair question. And we've all asked it. When life gets tough, when confusing things happen, it feels only human to respond *why?* That's what Moses said to God after Pharaoh increased the workload of the Israelite slaves and they, in turn, cursed Moses. Who can blame him? Most of us would have asked the same thing. *Why, God? Why?*

But in Exodus 6:1-8, God doesn't answer Moses' question. Instead he answers a different question: *Who?* God draws Moses' focus off the daunting circumstances in his life and onto God's identity. God says "I am Yahweh—'the LORD'" (v. 2), and he reminds Moses that he is the God of the patriarchs.

God's words here mirror what he told Moses at the burning bush: "I AM WHO I AM. Say this to the people of Israel: I AM has sent me to you . . . Say this to the people of Israel: Yahweh, the God of your ancestors—the God of Abraham, the God of Isaac, and the God of Jacob—has sent me to you" (Exodus 3:14, 15).

"I Am Who I Am" has been translated in different ways, including "I Am That I Am," "I Will Be What I Will Be," and "I Am He Who Is." God uses this holy name in Exodus 6 as if to say to Moses that knowing him as the I Am, the one true God, is all the answer Moses really needs.

The same is true for us. When we are confused or afraid or frustrated, God's answer is often not telling us "why" and explaining his plans. God's answer to us is: I Am.

Where's *your* focus? How easily is your attention drawn away from God and onto the circumstances of your life? And what question consumes you during the difficult times of your life: *why?* or *who?* When the going gets tough, it's very easy to lose perspective and get caught up and dragged down by everything that appears to be going wrong. But *God* is all the answer you need. As you focus on him—on knowing him, experiencing his presence, worshiping him—you'll find courage to face the hurdles before you. You'll know that God is the constant—the I Am—no matter what else changes in your life.

In preparation for leading this small group session, pray: God, you are the I Am. You are the one true God. You are the center of my life and the focus of my heart. Please help me not to be distracted by the circumstances that surround me or the discouragement that sometimes threatens to overtake me. Give me the steady courage to trust in you with consistency and determination. Help me to know you more and more, each and every day.

Lord, please help my jr. highers as I challenge them to keep their focus on who you are. They are at an age where it is very easy to get distracted. Please speak through me as I help them study your Word. In your name: the great I Am. Amen.

The Session

Rearrange or delete sections of the study to best meet your group's needs.

b4 u meet

A couple of days before your group meets, send a text message to your kids reminding them of the upcoming Connect study. (If some teens don't text, send them an e-mail or a message on Facebook or MySpace.)

txt a frnd `about 5 minutes`

Invite your small group to consider this question:

✸ When you have a huge task to do (finishing a big school project, concentrating during a test, doing your best during a huge competition, etc.), what helps you stay focused?

When they've got an answer, invite them to get out their cell phones and text their answer to another person in the room. (If kids don't have their own phone, they could borrow a friend's or could form pairs and talk about their answer to this question.)

When you're ready to move on to the next part of the study, have them put their cell phones away for now. ✸

mic check `about 5 minutes`

Before your session, you will have printed off different optical illusions you found online. Spread them around the room and invite teens to look at them all.

After a few minutes, have everyone gather together as a large group. Gather all the images in front of you and ask them to vote on the best ones. Ask them why they picked those favorites.

Then say something like this: The key to most optical illusions is focus. They trick your brain by drawing the focus of your eyes to particular areas on the image. And when our focus is off, our perception of what we're seeing gets distorted. That's a lot like real life. 🌟

solo about 5 minutes

solo/strike a chord handout

Tell your jr. highers you'd like them to find a spot in your meeting area where they can be alone and spend about 5 minutes reading Scripture and thinking about what it means. Remind them that in your past sessions, you've read about Moses' mission from God, but how it didn't start out so great—neither Pharaoh nor the Israelites reacted how Moses expected. Pharaoh made life for the Hebrew slaves even worse, and the people got ticked at Moses! Now they'll look at how Moses responded to God about this rejection.

Give each teen a copy of the **solo/strike a chord** handout and a pen or pencil, inviting them to read and follow the instructions. (Have them read through only the top portion, **solo**, right now, and they'll need the **strike a chord** portion in a few minutes.) Here's a copy of what they'll read:

Take 5 minutes to read Exodus 5:22–6:8. Consider:
🌟 What question does Moses ask?
🌟 Does God answer his question, or does he give him something else to think about?

When the kids understand what they're supposed to do, have them take off and find a spot to read and reflect. After about 5 minutes, call everybody back together. 🌟

freestyle `about 10 minutes`

Tell the group that before you discuss what God told Moses, you want to look at some ideas people have about God. Divide your students into 4 evenly sized groups (likely pairs or trios). Give each group 1 of the misperceptions about God from the "Misperceptions" handout you cut apart before the study. (Be sure to familiarize yourself with the "Misperceptions" handout so you can walk around and help assist discussion as needed.)

Give groups several minutes to read their assigned misperception description together and share their thoughts to the questions listed. Then have everyone gather back together and allow each group to explain their assigned misperception to everybody else and give a few thoughts about the questions they discussed.

Conclude this section of the session by saying something like: Now that we've looked at people's misperceptions about God, let's discuss what God says to Moses and see what God says about himself. ✤

strike a chord `about 15 minutes`

Communicate these thoughts to your students:

Misperceptions handout

hidden track

If you've got less than 8 participants (including yourself), form just 3 groups and discard 1 of the "Misperceptions" descriptions. If you've got less than 6 participants, form 2 groups and give each group 2 of the descriptions to read.

txt it

You may want to give your teens the option of texting their answers to these questions to you during your discussion time. Read out loud some of their answers and use them as springboards for further discussion.

solo/strike a chord handout

txt it

If you want, invite kids to answer these questions both by talking aloud and by texting. As some share their answers, others can text them to you. Read some of their thoughts aloud and build upon their ideas as your group explores these issues together.

We read during our **solo** time from Exodus 5:22–6:8 where Moses asks God, "Why? Why? Why?" Yet God answers Moses not by telling him the answer to "why" but instead tells him "who." God focused Moses on who God is—I Am.

Have the group now look at the bottom portion of the **solo/strike a chord** handout and use it to guide your small group Bible exploration and discussion together as a group. Here's a copy of the **strike a chord** text for you to use to guide your discussion time:

Look at Exodus 5:22–6:8 together and talk about these questions:

✦ Have you ever noticed the word Lord in the Bible written in small capital letters like that? What do you think that means?

Look back to when Moses first heard God from the burning bush. God explains his name there: Exodus 3:13-15. Read this passage with your group.

✦ Lord is translated "I Am Who I Am." You may have heard of Yahweh. This is the first time God has revealed this name for himself. What do you think he means by it?

✦ How do you think it made Moses feel to learn this new name? What hope or security or answers did that give to Moses? to the Israelites?

Finish up your discussion with the following:

✦ In Exodus 5:22–6:8, when Moses is sad and worried and scared and confused, God reminds Moses of what he said at the burning bush. He uses the same name for himself: Yahweh. "Focus, Moses," he's saying. "Remember all that I have done, Moses. I am faithful, good, true, and powerful. I am the God of your people, your ancestors. I will not let you down. Focus on *who I am.*"

✦ We can see that God is not distant—he is right there with Moses. And he gets directly involved; he hears the painful cries of the Israelite slaves, and he cares about their struggles. ✦

encore [about 5 minutes]

Say, There are many different opinions about God in the world, but there is only one true God, and here in the Bible God reveals to us who he is. He says to us, "I am Yahweh—I Am Who I Am."

Have your kids get another perspective of God by reading Psalm 139:1-18. Emphasize some of the powerful truths we can learn about God through this passage.

Drive home the session point with these ideas:

✦ I Am is the God who created the world, who performed miracles, who was faithful to his people throughout time, who came to earth as a man, who died on the cross for us, who forgives us of our sins, and who wants us to know him just as he wanted Moses to.

✦ When we focus on the hard circumstances in our lives, like fights with friends, problems with grades, frustrations about our appearance, problems on our sports team, discouragement about school, problems with our family, or worse, our perspective gets really distorted. Tough situations can take over all our thoughts and sap away our emotional energy. And we can end up whining, scared, doubting, or confused like Moses.

✱ We need to take our eyes off of all that tough stuff surrounding us and focus on who God is. When we know the I Am, we can face the challenges in our lives. ✱

playlist

To add some powerful ambiance to this worship experience, download these songs to your iPod (or to a CD) and play them (in this order) while kids create:
"Only True God" by Kathryn Scott
"How Great is Our God" by Chris Tomlin
"We're Amazed" by The Longing

backstage pass   about 10 minutes

Invite kids to take some time to respond to God through art. Point out the table of art supplies you've set out, and have them grab some paper and the supplies they want. Tell them to take the next few minutes to create an image that represents who God is to them.

They can do anything they'd like, such as drawing a symbol or a picture. Or perhaps they want to draw his name—I Am—or write other words describing him. They could do something very abstract to express what God is like.

Tell your kids that they don't need to show anyone what they create. It's something for *them* to keep, to help them remember to focus on who God is.

Prompt kids to spread out throughout the room and work on their artistic expressions. ✱

hit the road   about 2 minutes

Wrap up with prayer. But use this time to continue to focus on who God is. Have kids sit in a circle. Ask each jr. higher to pray aloud one short sentence prayer to God that begins with the words "You are . . ." For example, they might pray "You are trustworthy" or "You are personal." After a few minutes of praying, conclude by asking God to help each of you remain focused on who he is, the I Am.

Let your kids know you'll be sending **5 for 5 world tour** life application and devotional challenges for them to do each day via Twitter, e-mail, or through a Facebook group you've set up. (Or, if you prefer not to use these technology options, pass out copies of the **5 for 5 world tour** handout you've downloaded from the CD-ROM to the teens.) Encourage your kids to strive to spend about 5 minutes each day connecting with God through these devotional experiences.

Right after your meeting, send kids the first **5 for 5 world tour** challenge for them to do tomorrow via Twitter, e-mail, or by posting it on a Facebook page (or youth group Web page) you've set up. Continue to send 1 challenge each day for the 5 days following your meeting.

About 2 days after your group meets, send a text message to your kids, encouraging them to keep focusing on God. Prompt them to keep at it with their **5 for 5 world tour** challenges and let them know you're praying for them.

5 for 5 world tour handout

Feel-Good vs.
True Faith

The Prep

Session goal: Jr. highers will compare the false faith of Pharaoh to the true faith God wants them to exhibit in their lives.

Scriptures: Exodus 8:8, 28; Exodus 9:27; Exodus 10:16, 17; Exodus 11:4, 5; Exodus 12:3, 6-8, 12, 13, 28, 31, 32; Mark 9:17-24; John 3:18; John 4:48; John 6:29, 35, 36; John 9:35-38; John 11:25-27; John 14:10-12; John 16:29-31; John 17:20, 21; John 20:24-28; 1 Corinthians 5:7

You'll need:

* Bibles
* Pens or pencils
* 2 bowls or containers to pull slips of paper from

Download and print:

* "Unbelievable!"/"Jesus' definition of *believe*" handout (1 copy, cut into slips)
* **solo/strike a chord** discussion guide (1 per teen)
* "Sure, I Believe . . ." handout (1 per teen)
* "Nicene Creed" handout (1 per teen)

Optional supplies:

* For **backstage pass:** CD player and CD or iPod with recommended **playlist** songs.

✦ For **hit the road:** Download and print copies of this week's **5 for 5 world tour** take-home page (1 per teen) if you are unable to use the technology options.

Setting it up:

✦ Cut apart your "Unbelievable!"/"Jesus' definition of *believe*" hand-out into slips. In one pile, place all the "Unbelievable!" slips for **mic check**. You'll need 1 slip per teen (plus or 1 or 2 extra), making sure you have an even number of "make it up" and "tell the truth" slips. Fold each of those slips and place them all in a bowl or container. Cut up all the "Jesus' definition of *believe*" slips for **strike a chord**. Place these slips in a different bowl or container—no need to fold them.

✦ If you'd like to use the optional **playlist** recommendations, download the song "Nicene Creed" by Five Cent Stand and ready your iPod or burn a CD in order to play the song during the session.

Leader insight:

In the wake of tragic events, the TV news is filled with images of public figures and celebrities expressing hope in God, talking about prayer, or using Jesus' name (and not in vain!). Acknowledging God and calling out to him in times of trouble is a natural human response to fear and heartache. And in most of those cases, the rhetoric about God and faith was likely very sincere and well-meaning.

Another time God seems to show up on TV is during award shows or sporting events. At least a few times during award ceremonies or sports championships, the artists and athletes who win will publicly thank God for their victory. Sometimes these people are dedicated

Christians trying to share their faith, but other times the mention of God seems like mere lip service—especially if the song or film being awarded is full of immorality and profanity!

We see something similar in Pharaoh's reaction to the plagues God sends upon Egypt in Exodus 7–12. As God showed his power and authority, bringing misery upon the nation of Egypt, Pharaoh responded by acknowledging God. Pharaoh's nation faced tragedy after tragedy, so he expressed "belief" in this God of the Israelites, hoping to stop the onslaught against his country's economy and citizens.

But there are some important differences between Pharaoh's false faith and true belief in God. And the same is true of the popular and sentimental faith people proclaim to have in our culture that only seems to acknowledge God when it's convenient. In today's study, you'll help your kids examine and explore these differences. Jr. highers are growing up in a world where many of their peers (and many adults) claim to believe in God and *faith* is a feel-good term, but usually there is no connection to people's way of life. They'll compare Pharaoh's response to God with the Israelites who marked their doors with lamb's blood. They'll learn about the historic connection between the Passover and Christ's own sacrifice—how Jesus marks our *lives* with his blood.

What about you? How is your faith marking your life? Can people see by your words and actions that your belief in God is sincere, consistent, and life-changing? Is it at the very core of who you are? How does your commitment to Jesus stand in contrast to the fake, feel-good "faith" that permeates our culture? How do your words of truth help young people see the difference between convenient belief and lifelong dedication to Christ?

In preparation for leading this small group session, pray: God, I acknowledge that you are the one and only true God. I believe that you are the Lord of the universe and the Lord of my life. You are my master. Help me to grow more committed to you and more obedient to you. And help my kids understand what true belief in you really looks like. Give them wisdom and insight as we explore your Word together. Help them to discern the important difference between feel-good "faith" and a true commitment to you. Guide my words and my actions as I lead them through this session. In your name—Yahweh—amen.

The Session

Rearrange or delete sections of the study to best meet your group's needs.

txt a frnd `about 5 minutes`

Invite your small group to consider this question:

✦ What is something imaginary that you believed in when you were a little kid?

When they've got an answer, invite them to get out their cell phones and text their answer to another person in the room. (If kids don't have their own phone, they could borrow a friend's or could form pairs and talk about their answer to this question.)

When you're ready to move on to the next part of the study, have them put their cell phones away for now. ✦

mic check `about 5 to 10 minutes`

Explain to your group that you are going to tell each other unusual things about your lives—but some things will be real and some things fake. Each person is going to draw a slip of paper, and it will either say "tell the truth" or "make it up." Kids must obey the slip and either tell something strange that really happened or make up something to fool everyone.

b4 u meet

A couple of days before your group meets, send a text message to your kids reminding them of the upcoming Connect study. (If some teens don't text, send them an e-mail or a message on Facebook or MySpace.)

Unbelievable!/Jesus' definition of *believe* handout

For example, kids might say, "When I was a kid I used to lick frogs" or "I'm the only guy of all my siblings and cousins" or "My favorite food of all time is pizza with green olives." Make sure kids know that they only need to say a very short statement (like 1 sentence)—not tell an elaborate story. The rest of the group will then vote if they think the statement is real or fake.

When everyone understands, have kids draw their slips and keep them private so no one can see. Give kids 1 or 2 minutes to think of something and then have people share their statements. After each person makes his or her statement, ask the group to vote thumbs up or down whether they believe it's real or fake. Then have that person reveal if the statement was real or made up. You take a turn as well!

After everyone has finished, ask the group:

* Which fake statement was the most believable? Why?
* Which true statement was the most unbelievable? Why?

solo about 5 minutes

solo/strike a chord handout

Tell your jr. highers you'd like them to find a spot in your meeting area where they can be alone and spend about 5 minutes reading Scripture and thinking about what it means. Remind them that last week they looked at how God encouraged Moses to keep focusing on God. God revealed his name, Yahweh, I Am. Now they're going to look at some things Pharaoh said when the plagues came upon his land.

Give each teen a copy of the **solo/strike a chord** handout and a pen or pencil, inviting them to read and follow the instructions. (Have them read through only the top portion,

solo, right now, and they'll need the **strike a chord** portion in a few minutes.) Here's a copy of what they'll read:

Take 5 minutes to read Exodus 8:8, 28; Exodus 9:27; Exodus 10:16, 17; and Exodus 12:31, 32. Consider:

✦ Based on what you've just read, did Pharaoh believe in God? Why or why not?

When the kids understand what they're supposed to do, have them take off and find a spot to read and reflect. After about 5 minutes, call everybody back together. ✦

freestyle `about 10 minutes`

Begin by communicating these ideas to your group: We use the word *believe* in our culture in several different ways. For example, I believe this will work. I believe we may run into some trouble up ahead. I believe in gravity. I believe in Jesus.

People can use the word *believe* as a way of expressing hope or certainty in an outcome. People can say *believe* to claim something is real or true. Or people can use the term *believe* to indicate that they fully trust and give their allegiance to something or someone. We're interested in these last two definitions of *believe*—the idea that something is real or true and the idea of giving one's total trust and allegiance to something.

Give each teen a copy of the "Sure, I Believe" handout. Ask volunteers to read aloud the quotes from the celebrities listed on the page. Then ask:

Sure, I Believe handout

txt it

You may want to give your teens the option of texting their answers to these questions to you during your discussion time. Read out loud some of their answers and use them as springboards for further discussion.

✦ Do you think these people really believe in God? Why or why not?

✦ Name some situations when it's popular to believe in God or acknowledge him.

To get them started brainstorming on this question, you may want to bring up items from the **Leader insight** section: government people speaking about God during times of national tragedy, actors and musicians thanking God at awards ceremonies, sports players thanking God after winning, etc.

Talk to your kids about this: In our culture, it's very common for people to claim they believe in God or to say that they have faith. But it's a faith that seems to only come out at certain times. Most of the time, it appears to be nonexistent. We might call that *feel-good faith*.

Have kids take a minute or 2 to individually list some descriptions of feel-good vs. true faith on their handouts. After 1 or 2 minutes, ask the group to work together to come up with a description of feel-good faith and true faith. ✦

solo/strike a chord handout

strike a chord   about 15 to 20 minutes

Say, During your **solo** time, you read some things that Pharaoh said. Have the group now look at the bottom portion of the **solo/strike a chord** handout, and use it to guide your small group Bible exploration and discussion together as a group. Here's a copy of the **strike a chord** text for you to use to guide your discussion time:

Reread all or a few verses from Exodus 8:8, 28; Exodus 9:27; Exodus 10:16, 17; and Exodus 12: 31, 32 together, and talk about these questions:

✤ Do you think Pharaoh was showing true faith or just feel-good faith? Defend your answer.

✤ How do Pharaoh's statements compare with celebrities' statements about God that we hear today? How can we evaluate if people in the media are showing true or feel-good faith?

txt it

If you want, invite kids to answer these questions both by talking aloud and by texting. As some share their answers, others can text them to you. Read some of their thoughts aloud and build upon their ideas as your group explores these issues together.

Say something like this:

Pharaoh seems to believe that God is real. But he doesn't put his total trust in God—he doesn't honor God as the one true God; he doesn't adjust his life to line up with God's truth.

In Exodus 7 through 12, God sent plagues upon Egypt. Time and time again, through each plague, the message came through loud and clear: The God of the Israelites is the only true God. Though God made it abundantly clear that he alone is to be feared and worshiped, Pharaoh saw Yahweh as just one of many gods who he was trying to appease in order to get his way.

Let's compare Pharaoh's type of belief in God with the way the word *believe* is used by Jesus in the Gospel of John.

Have your kids get into pairs or trios, and invite each group to draw 2 slips from the "Jesus' definition of *believe*" slips. Instruct groups to read their Bible passages together, and then use them to come

hidden track

If you've got 3 or fewer groups of pairs/trios, have each group draw 3 slips.

up with a 1-sentence definition of the word *believe* based on their Scriptures.

Direct everyone to gather back together as a large group, and invite groups to read their definitions of belief based on the passages in John. Affirm kids as they read. Then, once all the definitions have been read, ask the group:

What sort of response does God want from those who truly believe? ⭐

encore · about 5 minutes

Say, During the final plague against Egypt, we see a demonstration of faith that stands in sharp contrast to Pharaoh's feel-good faith. We see an example of true faith.

Invite a few volunteers to read aloud an abbreviated version of the first Passover account by focusing on these selections: Exodus 11:4, 5; Exodus 12:3, 6-8, 12, 13, 28.

Recap the story by summarizing what has been read, then say, The Israelites didn't just believe God exists. They believed he was the one true God and he was to be worshiped and obeyed. And they marked their homes with the blood of slaughtered lambs. It was a visual, physical sign of their belief and their trust in God. Their faith was one of action; it was part of their identity. They believed God would protect and save them.

The Bible calls Jesus the Passover lamb. Read aloud 1 Corinthians 5:7, and have students

txt it

If you want, invite kids to answer these questions both by talking aloud and by texting. As some share their answers, others can text them to you. Read some of their thoughts aloud and build upon their ideas as your group explores these issues together.

follow along. Then say, Jesus was crucified for us. When we accept him into our hearts and commit our lives to him, it is as if we are covered by his blood. We are marked with his blood, like the doors of the Hebrews' homes. The punishment of death passes over us. We are saved by Jesus' sacrifice!

Ask: What does the Israelites' example show you about real faith? ⭐

backstage pass `about 5 minutes`

Pass out copies of "Nicene Creed" and explain that it's a statement of the central beliefs of the Christian faith that was written in the 4th century. Invite everyone to silently read through it, asking God to show them what it means to hold dear and to love God and his truths. Close by leading the group in saying the Nicene Creed in unison as a declarative prayer to God. ⭐

hit the road `about 1 minute`

We filled our study today by talking about the word *believe*. Believing in God and in his Word is so much more than just mental agreement with a set of facts. And it is so much more than just paying attention to him when it's convenient to us—like only when things are going really bad in our lives and we pray because we need help.

Nicene Creed handout

playlist

Help students prayerfully explore the meaning of the Nicene Creed before they pray it together by setting aside an extra 4 minutes for individual prayer as they listen to the song "Nicene Creed" by the band Five Cent Stand. After the song, lead your kids in praying the Creed together.

To prepare, download "Nicene Creed" by Five Cent Stand to your iPod (or burn a CD).

Right after your meeting, send kids the first **5 for 5 world tour** challenge for them to do tomorrow via Twitter, e-mail, or by posting it on a Facebook page (or youth group Web page) you've set up. Continue to send 1 challenge each day for the 5 days following your meeting.

About 2 days after your group meets, send a text message to your kids, encouraging them to live out their belief in God. Prompt them to keep at it with their **5 for 5 world tour** challenges and let them know you're praying for them.

5 for 5 world tour handout

Believing in God and his saving grace through Jesus is holding him dear—loving him with all that we are. It's making him the center of our being—making him the core of our lives. And when we do that, we respond to God by living out our faith. People can see in our actions that we are marked by God—we are living for him!

Do others know you are marked for him?

Let your kids know you'll be sending **5 for 5 world tour** life application and devotional challenges for them to do each day via Twitter, e-mail, or through a Facebook group you've set up. (Or, if you prefer not to use these technology options, pass out copies of the **5 for 5 world tour** handout you've downloaded from the CD-ROM to the teens.) Encourage your kids to strive to spend about 5 minutes each day connecting with God through these devotional experiences.

Daily Dependence

The Prep

Session goal: As they explore God's provision of manna for Moses and the Israelites, jr. highers will come to recognize their own need to depend on God day-by-day.

Scriptures: Exodus 16:1–17:7; Deuteronomy 8:3; Psalm 20:7; Psalm 42:1, 2; Matthew 4:4; Matthew 6:11; Acts 1:8; Ephesians 1:18-21

You'll need:

* Bibles
* Pens or pencils
* 2 large bowls
* Piggy bank
* 20 to 30 pennies (enough so each teen has 2)
* 1 large piece of roll paper
* Masking tape
* Colored markers
* Fresh, warm bread (or rolls)
* 1 garbage can
* Several permanent markers
* Bottled water (1 bottle per kid)
* Several battery-powered children's toys
* Working batteries (for the toys)
* Cell phone
* Paper, cut into strips
* Container with a lid (such as a coffee can)
* Stopwatch or clock with a second hand

Download and print:

* "Desert Survival Challenge" handout (1 per teen)
* **solo/strike a chord** discussion guide (1 per teen)
* "Exploration Stations" handout (1 copy, cut apart)

Optional supplies:

* For **backstage pass**: CD player and CD or iPod with recommended **playlist** songs.
* For **hit the road**: Download and print copies of this week's **5 for 5 world tour** take-home page (1 per teen) if you are unable to use the technology options.

Setting it up:

* Set up 6 "Exploration Stations" for the **freestyle** section of this session. Print off the handout "Exploration Stations" and cut up the paper to put instructions at each station. Here is the set-up for each station:

    Station 1: Fill a large bowl with the 20 to 30 pennies and place a piggy bank next to it.

    Station 2: Set out the roll paper on the ground (or tape it to a wall) and set markers on the floor in front of it. This will become a graffiti wall.

    Station 3: Set out some bread and a garbage can for clean-up.

    Station 4: Set out several permanent markers and bottled water. You'll need 1 bottle per kid.

    Station 5: Collect several fun battery-powered children's toys. Take out the batteries and set the toys out. Next to the toys, fill a bowl with the workable batteries that correspond with the toys. You should have enough batteries so that every toy can be turned on.

Station 6: Set out a cell phone, paper slips, pens, and the container with a lid. (If it's a disposable container like a coffee can, you may want to cut a slit in the lid for teens to slide in their papers.)

✦ If you'd like to use the optional **playlist** recommendations, download the songs "Ancient Voices" (the theme song from the *Survivor* TV show) for the **mic check** section and "Breathe" (also called "The Air I Breathe") for the **backstage pass** section. There are several Christian artists who've recorded "Breathe," and any will do. Ready your iPod or burn a CD in order to play the songs during the session.

Leader insight:

Imagine opening your refrigerator one morning, only to find moldy cheese, browned and smelly lettuce, curdled milk, and meat infected with maggots. Gross!

This is what some of the Israelites discovered when they tried to hoard manna, storing it up as a provision to ward off hunger in the future. It went rotten. It stank. It squirmed. God memorably showed them that their efforts to provide for themselves were utterly useless and repugnant.

When God provided manna and quail for his people in the desert, it was more than an act of love—it was a lesson in dependence. Unable to save food (except for the Sabbath), the Israelites were forced to go to sleep each night, knowing that the only way they'd eat tomorrow is if *God* provided food. There was no way they could trust in their own abilities; they *had* to rely entirely on God. And God set it up this way on purpose! "Yes, he humbled you by letting you go hungry and then feeding you with manna, a food previously unknown to you and your ancestors. He did it to teach you that people do not live by bread alone; rather, we live by every word that comes from the mouth of the LORD" (Deuteronomy 8:3).

Part of God's provision was the hunger itself—he fostered in the Israelites a sense of their need for him, their longing for him, and their humble position without him. Day in and day out, he taught them that he is their true source of sustenance and satisfaction.

Wow! What a powerful lesson for us today. In our world of self-esteem, self-reliance, self-confidence, self-actualization (etc., etc., etc.), we humans could use a good dose of humility! And even those of us who love God and seek to follow him with our lives can find ourselves caught up in the same mind-set as the Israelites who hoarded away manna: We desire to trust God but aren't really willing to *risk* anything for him; we give him lip service, but, in actuality, we depend a great deal on ourselves and often mentally take the credit for all that's going well in our lives.

What about you? How often do you really think about the truth that you are just as dependent upon God for sustenance and life as the Israelites were during those years in the desert? Do you live in a way that relies on him that much? Or—be honest, now—do you rely heavily on yourself and use God as your back-up plan when things go wrong? How can you connect with the real hunger of your soul—the hunger that rejects self and only finds true satisfaction in God himself?

In preparation for leading this small group session, pray: God, you are my daily bread. You are the oxygen of my soul. You are truly all that I need. I confess to you that I often lose sight of this truth. Humble me, Lord. Help me to live by your words, satisfied and fulfilled by you alone. Prepare my kids for how they'll encounter you through your Word, through hands-on experiences, and through conversations with each other. Touch each of their hearts; draw each of them closer to you. I pray these things in your name, Jesus Christ, the bread of life. Amen.

b4 u meet

A couple of days before your group meets, send a text message to your kids reminding them of the upcoming Connect study. (If some teens don't text, send them an e-mail or a message on Facebook or MySpace.)

The Session

Rearrange or delete sections of the study to best meet your group's needs.

txt a frnd `about 5 minutes`

Invite your small group to consider this question:

❋ If you were stranded on a desert island (with a good survival kit!) and you could have only 1 possession from home with you, what would you want to have? Why?

When they've got an answer, invite them to get out their cell phones and text their answer to another person in the room. (If kids don't have their own phone, they could borrow a friend's or could form pairs and talk about their answer to this question.)

When you're ready to move on to the next part of the study, have them put their cell phones away for now. ❋

Desert Survival Challenge handout

mic check `about 5 minutes`

Give each teen a pen and a copy of the "Desert Survival Challenge" handout. Have them determine what their top priorities would be if stranded in the desert. Give kids several minutes to complete the quiz (facts found on www.desertusa.com), and then share the correct answers to see which kid is most likely to survive.

Answers:
1. Water is #1, Fire is #2, Shelter is #3, Signals are #4, Food is #5.
2. False
3. True
4. Hair spray, extra pair of socks, gum, rehydrating sports drinks, duct tape

solo `about 5 minutes`

Tell your kids you'd like them to find a spot in your meeting area where they can be alone and spend about 5 minutes reading Scripture and thinking about what it means. Remind them that last week they read about the Israelites' true faith vs. Pharaoh's feel-good faith. But now we'll read how hard it was for them to maintain that faith when it came to depending on God daily.

Give each teen a copy of the **solo/strike a chord** handout and a pen or pencil, inviting them to read and follow the instructions. (Have them read through only the top portion, **solo**, right now, and they'll need the **strike a chord** portion in a few minutes.) Here's a copy of what they'll read:

Take 5 minutes to read Exodus 16:1-8, 13-32, 35 and Exodus 17:1-7. Consider:

✷ What stands out to you most from this passage? Why?

playlist #1

To add some fun ambiance to this activity, download the theme from the reality TV show *Survivor* to your iPod (or to a CD). There are several versions of this song, called "Ancient Voices" available on iTunes. Play the song on repeat as kids complete the Desert Survival Challenge.

solo/strike a chord handout

When the kids understand what they're supposed to do, have them take off and find a spot to read and reflect. After about 5 minutes, call everybody back together. ✦

strike a chord   about 10 minutes

solo/strike a chord handout

Begin by saying something like this: After leaving Egypt, the Israelites were pursued by the Egyptian army. God miraculously provided a way for them to escape by parting the Red Sea so they could cross, then crashing it down upon the pursuing Egyptians. And now, after all the miracles of the plagues and the Red Sea, Moses and the Israelites found themselves in the middle of a desert: no food, no water, and no comforts.

Have someone summarize the Scriptures they read during their **solo** time about the Israelites' complaining and grumbling. Then have the group now look at the bottom portion of the **solo/strike a chord** handout, and use it to guide your small group Bible exploration and discussion together as a group. Here's a copy of the **strike a chord** text for you to use to guide your discussion time:

Discuss Exodus 16:1-8, 13-32, 35 and Exodus 17:1-7 together with these questions:

✤ What does this story show us about the Israelites? What characteristics did they show? How does this compare to their faith we read about last week when they put the blood on their doors?

✤ What does this story show us about God and God's character traits?

Say something like: It's hard to believe, isn't it, that even after the awesome way God showed his power in Egypt, the Israelites complained and didn't trust him. It's hard to believe, isn't it, that even after he parted the Red Sea so they could cross on dry land, they didn't fully rely on him. It's hard to believe, isn't it, that even after God saved them from the mighty Egyptian army, they still acted so self-centered. It's hard to believe . . . but is it really?

Communicate these ideas to your group:

txt it

If you want, invite kids to answer these questions both by talking aloud and by texting. As some share their answers, others can text them to you. Read some of their thoughts aloud and build upon their ideas as your group explores these issues together.

* This story shows us what *we* are like. We may not like to admit it, but we are a lot like the Israelites. We complain and grumble and cop an attitude when life isn't just how we want it. We feel uncomfortable fully relying on him, so we try to plan and save and come up with our own pitiful ways to solve the problems in our lives.

* We see a memorable way God taught the Israelites to rely on him: He prevented them from relying on themselves. By causing the food to rot and not letting them store food away, God made them trust him each and every day to provide. They *couldn't* rely on themselves, no matter how much they tried! Each day they had to wake up and know that the only way they'd eat any food would be if God gave it to them.

* This is the same idea of an important line from The Lord's Prayer. Jesus said to pray "Give us today the food we need" (Matthew 6:11). Jesus wants us to remember that we rely on God's provision *daily*.

* Read aloud Deuteronomy 8:3, then tell your kids that we all need to learn this same lesson. God will meet our needs, and our role is to rely on him in trust instead of relying on ourselves. We need

to realize that God is the source of our life—without him, we're nothing.

✦ This story also shows us what *God* is like. God is our provider. He didn't lead the Israelites out into the desert to die! He had a way to provide for them! And God is the same today: He is all-powerful, reliable, loving, and trustworthy. God is our provider, who sustains us and blesses us. God knows our deepest needs, and he offers to meet them. ✦

Exploration Stations handout

hidden track

If you need to shorten this activity, you may choose to have kids only visit 4 out of the 6 stations.

freestyle · about 20 to 30 minutes

Point out the 6 Exploration Stations you've set up around the room, and explain that teens will now have some time to creatively pray, worship, and explore Scripture on their own. Let them know that they'll form pairs and travel throughout the room, following the printed instructions at each station. The activities at each station should take about 5 minutes if kids don't rush through them.

Let pairs know that they can visit the stations in any order they'd like. The only 2 rules are: 1. They should stay on task with whatever they're supposed to do or discuss at each station, and 2. They shouldn't bother or distract other kids. When everyone understands, let them get started.

Here's a quick overview of what the kids will be doing at each station:

Station 1: Kids will put pennies in a piggy bank to launch a discussion about how some Israelites attempted to save manna. They'll consider what it means to truly rely on God.

Station 2: Kids will hold their breath, then think about how much they need God, moment by moment. They'll write down specific ways God meets their needs and provides for them.

Station 3: Teens will eat fresh bread and consider what it means to hunger for God.

Station 4: Kids will drink water and talk with each other about ways God satisfies their spiritual thirst.

Station 5: Teens will play with battery-operated toys and discuss what it means to live with God as one's power source.

Station 6: Kids will think about the importance of having constant communication with God and will write a short prayer.

hidden track

You may want to keep an eye on kids who may take the breath-holding activity in Station 2 too far. You don't want anyone passing out!

txt it

If you want, invite kids to answer these questions both by talking aloud and by texting. Read some of their thoughts aloud.

During the activity, wander around the room to help students with questions and to generally encourage teens to stay focused on what they're supposed to be doing. Give pairs a 10-minute and 5-minute warning as the exploration time draws to a close. When time's up, have everyone gather back together as a large group in the center of your meeting area. ✸

encore   about 5 minutes

Ask the group:
✸ Which station personally challenged you the most? Why?

✦ How did God speak to you during these experiences?

Affirm kids for what they've just shared with the group, then say something like this:

Even when we love God and we commit our lives to him, it's still very easy to slip into the habit of going through life without truly depending on him. Unless a tragedy strikes or we're facing a big challenge, we can often go through a whole day without recognizing that we need God desperately. We can go through a whole day without thinking about the truth that we're alive because of God—every breath, every heartbeat is given to us by him.

Reread Deuteronomy 8:3, then say, I hope these experiences have helped you to learn the same truth that the Israelites did: We don't live by our own strength alone. We live because of God, who is our true and trustworthy provider. And it is only in God that we can find true satisfaction in life. ✦

backstage pass & hit the road about 5 minutes

Ask kids to spread out throughout the room, sit comfortably, and close their eyes. Challenge them to listen to the words of the song you are about to play and to pray about what they mean. If you're able, dim the lights. Then play the song "Breathe" while kids pray.

When the song is done, wrap up with a simple prayer of dedication, asking God to help your kids trust him as their provider and depend daily upon him for all their needs.

Let your kids know you'll be sending 5 for 5 world tour life application and devotional challenges for them to do each day via

Twitter, e-mail, or through a Facebook group you've set up. (Or, if you prefer not to use these technology options, pass out copies of the **5 for 5 world tour** handout you've downloaded from the CD-ROM to the teens.) Encourage your kids to strive to spend about 5 minutes each day connecting with God through these devotional experiences. 🌟

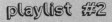
playlist #2

For this closing activity, you will need to download the song "Breathe" (or called "This Is the Air I Breathe") to your iPod (or to a CD) and play it while students pray. There are several versions of this song available.

5 for 5 world tour handout

aftr u meet

Right after your meeting, send kids the first **5 for 5 world tour** challenge for them to do tomorrow via Twitter, e-mail, or by posting it on a Facebook page (or youth group Web page) you've set up. Continue to send 1 challenge each day for the 5 days following your meeting.

About 2 days after your group meets, send a text message to your kids, encouraging them to thank God for what he provides daily. Prompt them to keep at it with their **5 for 5 world tour** challenges and let them know you're praying for them.

7

Always with Us

The Prep

Session goal: As jr. highers examine the accounts of God's presence with Moses and the Israelites, they'll be challenged to have an awareness of God's presence in every moment of their own lives.

Scriptures: Exodus 13:21, 22; Exodus 19:9; Exodus 33:12-14; Exodus 40:34-38; Deuteronomy 31:6; Psalm 139:7-10; Isaiah 43:1, 2; Matthew 28:20

You'll need:

* Bibles
* Pens or pencils

Download and print:

* **solo/strike a chord** discussion guide (1 per teen)
* "Journaling part 1" handout (1 per teen)
* "Journaling part 2" handout (1 per teen, but you may want to print/photocopy this on the back side of "Journaling part 1")

Optional supplies:

* For **backstage pass:** CD player and CD or iPod with recommended **playlist** songs.
* For **hit the road:** Download and print copies of this week's **5 for 5 world tour** take-home page (1 per teen) if you are unable to use the technology options.

Setting it up:

✦ If you are doing both the **freestyle** and **backstage pass** sections, you may want to print/photocopy "Journaling part 1" and "Journaling part 2" on the front/back of the same page for kids so you are only using 1 sheet for both activities.

✦ If you'd like to use the optional **playlist** recommendations, download the songs "Alone" by Ben Harper and the Innocent Criminals and "Never Alone" by BarlowGirl and ready your iPod or burn a CD in order to play the songs during the session.

Leader insight:

For the Israelites and Moses traveling in the desert, God was anything but hidden. A huge, towering reminder of his presence stood before them during the day: a pillar of cloud. An even more striking visual appeared at night: a pillar of brilliant fire! This is just one instance of many recorded in Exodus in which God reminded the Israelites that he was present with them.

For us today, the situation is a bit different. Scripture assures us, time and time again, of God's constant presence with us. We know that as followers of Jesus we have the Holy Spirit in our hearts. Yet we cannot *see* him—we don't get to witness sights like a pillar of fire or a cloud of God's glory descending on the tabernacle. And our feelings can often deceive us, causing us to lose sight of the awesome truth—prompting us to feel lonely, as if we're on our own in this world. Even the strongest of Christians have had times in which they've felt deeply and sorrowfully isolated and alone.

Grasping onto the truth that God's presence is with us every moment can transform our own spiritual growth and the growth of our jr. highers. Brother Lawrence, a French monk in the 1600s, called this "practicing God's presence." In the same way that we practice other spiritual disciplines, we train our hearts to form a habitual awareness of the spiritual reality that God is with us. In this sense, we are "praying continually" as Paul urged the Thessalonians to do (see 1 Thessalonians 5:17, *NIV*). With eyes open, going about our business, we can maintain a secret, silent conversation with our constant, faithful friend: Jesus.

What about you? How often do you focus your heart on God's presence? How encouraging would it be for you to have an ongoing, private conversation in your heart with God throughout the day? How much more empowered would you feel if you faced life fully aware of the truth that the Holy Spirit is within you, guiding you, gifting you, and leading you? How could this help you deal with feelings of loneliness or discouragement? What practical steps can you take to tune in your heart to God's steady presence?

In preparation for leading this small group session, pray: Holy Spirit, you are with me right now, in this moment. Help me develop a constant awareness of your presence with me. Just as you guided the Israelites and reassured them of your presence with clouds and fire, guide each step I take. And Lord, my jr. highers need to know and understand this truth. They are at an age filled with feelings of loneliness and isolation. Please use your Word and my teaching to help them know that they aren't alone. Comfort them with the truth that you are always with them and you are always available to talk and to listen. Inspire them to be more connected with you in each moment. Thank you for being here with us. In Jesus' name, amen. 🍂

A couple of days before your group meets, send a text message to your kids reminding them of the upcoming Connect study. (If some teens don't text, send them an e-mail or a message on Facebook or MySpace.)

The Session

Rearrange or delete sections of the study to best meet your group's needs.

txt a frnd · about 5 minutes

Invite your small group to consider this question:

✦ Who was your best friend as a child? What did you like to do together?

When they've got an answer, invite them to get out their cell phones and text their answer to another person in the room. (If kids don't have their own phone, they could borrow a friend's or could form pairs and talk about their answer to this question.)

When you're ready to move on to the next part of the study, have them put their cell phones away for now. ✦

mic check (option 1) · about 10 minutes

Lead everyone in playing the classic game Sardines. Sardines is a twist on Hide-n-Seek; instead of everyone hiding and 1 person looking, Sardines begins with 1 person hiding while everyone else looks.

Here's how it works: Turn the lights off or low in the area you've designated for the game and send a volunteer to hide. (Or you may choose to try this outside.) Lead everyone else in counting to 50 or 100, enough time for the kid to hide.

Then send everyone searching. The group should silently try to find the hiding person. If they do, their job is to try to hide *with* the hider. The goal of the game is for everyone to eventually find the

large group of people hiding together, often packed into a small space like sardines.

Play 1 or more rounds for 10 minutes. Afterward, ask whoever was it: What did it feel like to be alone? What did it feel like to be found by others? Ask the group: How did you feel as you searched, alone and in the dark? What was your reaction to finding everybody else and joining the group?

Then say, Being alone is not the same as feeling lonely. You may be alone and be just fine. But you also may be in a huge crowd of people yet feel alone. Everyone feels lonely at some point. But today we're going to talk about how we've never really alone because God is with us. ✦

hidden track

There are 2 **mic check** options for you. Pick the activity that best fits your group and meeting space.

mic check (option 2)   about 5 minutes

Start some conversation. Ask your kids:
✦ Would you ever go to a movie alone?
✦ Would you ever go out to eat by yourself?
✦ Would you go to a concert if no one else could go with you?
✦ Would you still go to an amusement park if everyone else cancelled?
✦ How far have you ever traveled by yourself?
✦ When you want to be alone, what is your favorite spot?

Then say something like this: You may have noticed a theme to these questions. They all involve being alone. But being alone is not the same as feeling lonely. You may be alone and be just fine. But you also may be in a huge crowd of people yet feel alone. If you wish, share a time when you have felt alone.

Then communicate these ideas to your group:

* Jr. high is a stage of life when loneliness can be a huge issue. You may not feel like your parents really know you or understand you like they once did. Your friendships are really important to you, and when those friends let you down, it can really hurt. Or you might feel lonely because a guy or a girl you like doesn't feel the same way about you. Or maybe someone at school has said something mean to you that made you feel isolated and alone.

* Everybody deals with loneliness at some point. It's tough to feel like no one really knows us or understands us or deeply cares about us. But today we're going to talk about how we're never really alone because God is with us.

solo/strike a chord handout

solo   about 5 minutes

Tell your kids you'd like them to find a spot in your meeting area where they can be alone and spend about 5 minutes reading Scripture and thinking about what it means.

Remind them that last week they read about the Israelites' daily dependence upon God. Now they'll read the ways God reminded his people that he was with them.

Give each teen a copy of the **solo/strike a chord** handout and a pen or pencil, inviting them to read and follow the instructions. (Have them read through only the top portion, **solo**, right now, and they'll need the **strike a chord** portion in a few minutes.) Here's a copy of what they'll read:

Take 5 minutes to read Exodus 13:21, 22; Exodus 19:9; and Exodus 40:34-38. Consider:

* What stands out to you most from this passage? Why?
* What visual reminder do you wish God would give you today?

When the kids understand what they're supposed to do, have them take off and find a spot to read and reflect. ✷

freestyle `about 5 minutes`

Pass out the "Journaling part 1" handout and pens. Invite kids to find a spot in the room to take a few minutes to think about and privately journal their thoughts about the journal prompt questions. When time's up, have kids fold up their papers and hold on to them for later in the study. ✷

strike a chord `about 15 minutes`

Say something like this: You just took some time to journal about loneliness. Though we all feel lonely at times, the truth of the matter is that if we have a relationship with God, we are never, ever alone. God is present with his people! Let's look at how God reassured his people of his presence with them during the time of Moses.

hidden track

If you are doing the **freestyle** section next, have students remain spread out for that activity.

Journaling part 1 handout

hidden track

If you just did the **solo** section, have kids remain spread out for this activity.

playlist

To help kids reflect on loneliness, download the song "Alone" by Ben Harper and the Innocent Criminals to your iPod (or to a CD) and play it as students write.

solo/strike a chord handout

Have the group now look at the bottom portion of the **solo/strike a chord** handout and use it to guide your small group Bible exploration and discussion together as a group. Here's a copy of the **strike a chord** text for you to use to guide your discussion time:

Reread Exodus 13:21, 22; Exodus 19:9; and Exodus 40:34-38 together and talk about these questions:

✦ What difference do you think it might have made to the Israelites to see these visual reminders of God's presence?

✦ Would it make a difference to you if you could see a miracle like that reminding you that God is with you? Why or why not?

✦ Do you think having faith in God is harder or easier for us than it was for the Israelites? Explain your answer.

Communicate these ideas to your group: Sometimes we may feel a little jealous of the Israelites—they had this huge, amazing visual reminder every moment that God was present with them. We don't have that visual to reassure us. But you know what? We have the same promise. If we have committed our lives to Jesus, God is with us in every moment, leading every step. We cannot see him, but we can know deep in our heart that it is true. When we face the choices and challenges of everyday life, God is with us.

txt it

If you want, invite kids to answer these questions both by talking aloud and by texting. As some share their answers, others can text them to you. Read some of their thoughts aloud and build upon their ideas as your group explores this topic together.

Invite a volunteer to read aloud Exodus 33:12-14. Explain that here we see a glimpse into Moses' heart. Though he's led the Israelites out of Egypt, he still has worries and fears. He wants to be a good leader, but he needs God's help. He wants to know how to live the way God wants. And God's reassurance to him is very simple: I am with you. God's presence with Moses will give him peace and rest as he faces the challenges ahead.

Prompt kids to take a few moments to read the following verses in their own Bibles: Deuteronomy 31:6 and Matthew 28:20. When they're done, let them know that God never abandons us. God never leaves us in the dark, all alone. God is always with us. Now this doesn't mean we will never *feel* lonely or alone! Sometimes faith means facing off with our feelings and saying, "Yes, I might feel lonely, but I know the truth: I am *not* alone." ✨

backstage pass · about 5 to 10 minutes

Pass out the "Journaling part 2" handout (or you may have printed it on the back of "Journaling part 1," which the kids already have) and pens. Invite kids to take their Bibles with them and find a spot in the room to take a few minutes to read the Scriptures listed on the page and respond to the journal prompt questions there. When time's up, have kids fold up their papers and slip them in their Bibles to take home. ✨

Journaling part 2 handout

playlist

To help kids reflect on the truth that God is always with them, download the song "Never Alone" by BarlowGirl to your iPod (or to a CD) and play it as they journal.

encore   about 5 minutes

Describe this true story to your group:

✤ There was a monk who lived in France in the 1600s. His name was Brother Lawrence, and one of his duties in his monastery was to work in the kitchen as the cook and dishwasher.

✤ All the monks had special times set aside throughout the day for prayer and devotions. They'd go to their rooms to be alone with God and to seek to know him better. Brother Lawrence enjoyed those times, but those weren't the moments when he felt closest to God. It wasn't in the times set aside for worship and prayer and spiritual things that he felt close to God—it was when he was washing dishes!

✤ Brother Lawrence was focused on the truth that God was always with him, in every moment. He loved to interact with God in the moments of everyday life—when cooking, when cleaning, when talking with friends. He called it "practicing God's presence." What this means is that he *practiced* constantly reminding himself that God was present with him. He described it pretty simply: He just paid attention to the reality that God was there! And he tried to fill his mind with loving thoughts toward God as he talked with God throughout the day. He didn't pray just at certain times—he was *always* praying by having an ongoing conversation with God.

✤ What a concept! The problem for most of us is that we often just don't think about God all day long—we get so caught up in the events of our day that we seldom think about God's presence with us.

Ask your group: What could it look like for you to "practice God's presence"? What would it take for you to be more aware of God's presence with you all the time?

Maybe it means that as you walk to your next class, you talk to God in your mind about your worries or concerns. Maybe you say

short silent prayers throughout the day, like "God, help me pay attention in this class" or "I love you, God" or "Thanks for that awesome sunset" or "Help me respect my parents, right now—they're driving me nuts" or "Forgive me for being so selfish."

Like God's people had a pillar of cloud and a pillar of fire to look at to remind them that God was with them, maybe you can give yourself visual reminders to help you pay closer attention to the truth that God is with you. You can put a Bible verse up in your locker or tie something onto your shoelace that will help you think about God when you see it.

Invite kids to share other ideas they have for practicing God's presence. ✦

hit the road `about 1 minute`

Read aloud Exodus 33:14: "The LORD replied, 'I will personally go with you, Moses, and I will give you rest—everything will be fine for you.'"

And Deuteronomy 31:6: "The LORD your God will personally go ahead of you. He will neither fail you nor abandon you."

And Matthew 28:20: "And be sure of this: I am with you always, even to the end of the age."

Say, God's promise to Moses and Joshua and the disciples are the same for you today.

txt it

If you want, invite kids to answer these questions both by talking aloud and by texting.

5 for 5 world tour handout

aftr u meet

Right after your meeting, send kids the first **5 for 5 world tour** challenge for them to do tomorrow via Twitter, e-mail, or by posting it on a Facebook page (or youth group Web page) you've set up. Continue to send 1 challenge each day for the 5 days following your meeting.

About 2 days after your group meets, send a text message to your kids, encouraging them to practice God's presence this week. Prompt them to keep at it with their **5 for 5 world tour** challenges and let them know you're praying for them.

Let this truth sink into your hearts each moment of each day of the coming week.

Let your kids know you'll be sending **5 for 5 world tour** life application and devotional challenges for them to do each day via Twitter, e-mail, or through a Facebook group you've set up. (Or, if you prefer not to use these technology options, pass out copies of the **5 for 5 world tour** handout you've downloaded from the CD-ROM to the teens.) Encourage your kids to strive to spend about 5 minutes each day connecting with God through these devotional experiences.

Never Forget

The Prep

Session goal: Jr. highers will examine the bad example of the Israelites' forgetfulness and will be inspired to live lives of faithful remembrance.

Scriptures: Exodus 20:4-6; Exodus 32:1-14; Deuteronomy 6:4-9; Psalm 77:11-20; Psalm 106:7-22; Psalm 136

You'll need:

* Bibles
* Pens or pencils
* 3 containers of toothpicks
* 3 bags of mini-marshmallows
* 3 large, flat pieces of cardboard
* Markers
* Long strips of plain paper that can be rolled into scrolls (1 per teen)
* Ribbons or rubber bands (1 per teen)

Download and print:

* **solo/strike a chord** discussion guide (1 per teen)
* "Come Thou Fount" handout (1 per teen)
* "What He's Done" handout (1 per teen)

Optional supplies:

* For **backstage pass:** CD player and CD or iPod with recommended **playlist** songs.

✹ For **hit the road:** Download and print copies of this week's **5 for 5 world tour** take-home page (1 per kid) if you are unable to use the technology options.

Setting it up:

✹ Create a model of something using 1 of your containers of toothpicks and 1 of your bags of mini-marshmallows and build it on 1 of your pieces of cardboard as a base. Your model could look like a house or a tower, a series of connected cubes, or anything you want. Just make sure it's architecturally sound enough to stay upright and together for the first activity. Place the model in a different room from your main meeting area.
✹ If you'd like to use the optional **playlist** recommendations, download the songs "Come Thou Fount" (sung by a number of artists—choose your favorite) and "Never Forget You" by Sonicflood and ready your iPod or burn a CD in order to play the songs during the session.

Leader insight:

The irony is anything but subtle.

Moses was up on Mount Sinai, and God had just finished giving him regulations about the Sabbath (Exodus 31:12-18). Along with all the other directions for worship, God wanted it to be clear to the Israelites that they were to set aside 1 full day every week to focus on remembering God. It was to be a day set aside for the purpose of resting—an entire day devoted to God and treated as holy. This was to be the rhythm of their life: 6 days working, the 7th day for God . . . over and over and over again. A pattern focused on remembering God and staying connected to him.

Meanwhile, the Israelites were down below *forgetting God*!

Exodus 32:1–33:6 tells the tragic story of the Hebrew people neglecting God's law, forgetting about his promises, and turning instead to a pagan practice of worship: crafting an idol. Despite all he had done, they turned away in disobedience! Despite his promises and his faithfulness, they forgot that God was with them, ever-present.

In this session, your jr. highers will explore the poignant and crucial themes of *forgetting* and *remembering* in Scripture. They'll learn the importance of constantly striving to remind themselves of God's faithfulness and their role of obedience to him. They'll discover that *remembering* God means loving him with all that they are: heart, soul, and strength.

What about you? Do you find yourself easily forgetting the great things God has done in your life? Could you name his many blessings in your life over the past year pretty quickly, or would you have to think about it a bit? If your answer is the latter, then maybe you need to spend more time intentionally remembering what God has done for you. Like the Israelites, we are all prone to wander—we all have a tendency to forget. What practical strategies can you implement to help you keep Christ ever before you, foremost in your thoughts and the Lord of all your actions?

In preparation for leading this small group session, pray: God, forgive me for forgetting about you. Forgive me for taking you for granted. Forgive me for my habits of inattentiveness. I ask that you'll inspire my kids as they look at the poor example of the Israelite's idolatry and forgetfulness; help them to honestly see their own tendency to neglect you. May they put effort into remembering you, worshiping you, and thanking you. Help us all, mighty God, to remember you always and love you with all that we are. Amen.

The Session

Rearrange or delete sections of the study to best meet your group's needs.

txt a frnd `about 5 minutes`

Invite your small group to consider this question:

✸ What's one embarrassing moment you've had that you wish you could forget?

When they've got an answer, invite them to get out their cell phones and text their answer to another person in the room. (If kids don't have their own phone, they could borrow a friend's or could form pairs and talk about their answer to this question.)

When you're ready to move on to the next part of the study, have them put their cell phones away for now. ✸

mic check `about 10 minutes`

Divide kids into 2 teams, and give each team a box of toothpicks, a bag of mini-marsh-mallows, and a large piece of cardboard (to serve as the base). Have teams spread apart so they don't watch each other work.

✸ Explain that you've created a model out of toothpicks and marshmallows. Both teams will try to create an exact replica of the model. Here's the catch: Only 1 person from each team can go look at the model. In other

b4 u meet

A couple of days before your group meets, send a text message to your kids reminding them of the upcoming Connect study. (If some teens don't text, send them an e-mail or a message on Facebook or MySpace.)

hidden track

In the **Setting it up** section in **The Prep** part of this session, you were instructed to build a model for this activity. Have this ready and sitting in another room near your meeting space.

hidden track

You may want to be sure that the representatives don't have their cell phones with them so that they can't take a photo of your model and ruin the point of the game!

words, they're building their replicas based on how well these team members can remember!

✦ Tell teams to choose their representatives (and they may want to pick people with good memories!), and then walk the 2 kids to the model to look. Let them look for 30 seconds. Then they must run back to the group and explain what they saw.

After a few minutes of working, allow a person from each team to go look at the model again. The team may choose to have the same person go back and look or have a new person look. Give these 2 kids 30 seconds to look, and then have them communicate back to the group more about the model.

After some time, call an end to the building and bring your model into the room and judge which team's project most closely resembles yours. Affirm all the kids for their efforts.

Ask the people who looked at the model: Was it harder or easier than you thought it would be to remember the details of this model? Why? In everyday life, do you consider yourself to have a good memory, a so-so memory, or a bad memory?

Then ask everyone whether they have a good, so-so, or bad memory. Tell your jr. highers that today you're going to see how having a bad memory led to a lot of trouble. ✦

solo/strike a chord handout

solo   about 5 minutes

Tell your kids you'd like them to find a spot in your meeting area where they can be alone and spend about 5 minutes reading Scripture and thinking about what it means.

Remind them that last week they read about the ways God visually reminded his people that he was present with them. Even though the Israelites had such wonders to remind them, they'll now read about when the Hebrew people surprisingly forgot about God.

Give each teen a copy of the **solo/strike a chord** handout and a pen or pencil, inviting them to read and follow the instructions. (Have them read through only the top portion, **solo**, right now, and they'll need the **strike a chord** portion in a few minutes.) Here's a copy of what they'll read:

Take 5 minutes to read Exodus 20:4-6 and Exodus 32:1-14. Consider:
✦ What stands out to you most from this passage? Why?
✦ Imagine how hurt God must have felt to watch the people he rescued turn from his love.

When the kids understand what they're supposed to do, have them take off and find a spot to read and reflect. After about 5 minutes, call everybody back together.

strike a chord about 15 minutes

Tell your group: During the past 7 weeks of our study, we've learned a lot of amazing things God did in the life of Moses and the Israelites. Since in this session we're talking about memory and not forgetting God, let's see if we can remember all the important highlights of the story so far. See how many things they can recall. Then say: God showed his people over

solo/strike a chord handout

txt it

If you want, invite kids to answer these questions both by talking aloud and by texting. As some share their answers, others can text them to you. Read some of their thoughts aloud and build upon their ideas as your group explores this topic together.

and over and over again that he was powerful, trustworthy, and present with them. But how did they respond?

Read aloud Psalm 106:7-22. Despite all God had done, the Israelites were forgetful. And as they forgot these truths about God, they began to whine and complain, their perspective got distorted, and they made sinful choices.

Have the group now look at the bottom portion of the **solo/strike a chord** handout, and use it to guide your small group Bible exploration and discussion together as a group. Here's a copy of the **strike a chord** text for you to use to guide your discussion time:

Discuss Exodus 20:4-6 and Exodus 32:1-14 together and talk about these questions:

✸ After Yahweh has miraculously delivered the Israelites from the hand of Pharaoh and intense slave labor in Egypt, why do you think they would ask Aaron for a golden calf? And why would Aaron comply with their request?

✸ What do you think the calf represented? Why was it so wrong?

✸ Why was God so angry with them?

Say: When you read this Scripture, don't you just want to yell at them, "What are you doing?! Why are you making an idol?!"

We don't know for certain why the Israelites created the golden calf. It could have been because they had lost sight of God's comforting presence, and somehow they felt like they'd lost their access to God. Or it could have been that they just wanted to worship in the way other nations did.

Either way, we can see that they'd totally forgotten God and his role in their lives! Instead of obeying him, they did their own thing. Instead of trusting him, they rushed ahead with their own plans. Despite all he had done for them, they responded with disobedience.

It's natural to judge the Israelites when we read this story. But we need to ask ourselves a tough question: Are we ever like them? Do we forget about God and all he has done for us? ✤

backstage pass about 5 minutes

Pass out copies of the "Come Thou Fount" handout along with pens. Invite students to read the words and listen to the music. Prompt them to circle words or phrases in the song that they relate to. Invite them to also jot down their thoughts on the back of the paper as they reflect on these questions:

✤ How often do I forget about God?

✤ Am I "prone to wander" like the Israelites were? ✤

encore about 5 minutes

Ask your group:

✤ What methods do you usually use to help yourself remember things?

✤ How do you remember phone numbers or birthdays?

✤ How do you remember information for tests?

Come Thou Fount handout

playlist

To help teens prayerfully consider their own forgetfulness and wandering nature, download the song "Come Thou Fount" (sung by a number of artists—choose your favorite) to your iPod (or to a CD) and play it while kids read the lyrics.

txt it

You may want to give your teens the option of texting their answers to these questions to you during your discussion time. Read out loud some of their answers and use them as springboards for further discussion.

Ask a volunteer to read aloud Deuteronomy 6:4-9 while everybody else reads along. Explain that this is a very moving passage that tells us what *remembering* God really looks like. This Scripture is still extremely important to Jewish people today. Some orthodox Jews practice these commandments very literally. They keep a small scroll of this Scripture on the doorpost of their house; it is called a *mezuzah*. They also wrap prayer bands upon their left arm and on their forehead called *phylacteries*. These bands have small, leather cubes on them that contain the text of this Bible passage.

Communicate to your group that the methods described in this passage would really help someone remember God: talking at home about God and his commands all the time, using symbols and physical reminders to think of him, writing down the words of Scripture, posting the words as reminders. And whether we use these specific methods from the Old Testament or others, the idea here is that we are to do everything we can to remember God. We are to do all that we can to remind ourselves constantly of God's loving power and faithful presence.

Ask: What are some practical things we can do to help us remember God in our everyday lives?

What He's Done handout

freestyle   about 5 to 10 minutes

Have your kids work in pairs or trios. Pass out copies of the "What He's Done" handout and some pens. Say: Let's take some time right now to remind ourselves of what God has done.

Prompt them to follow the instructions on the handout. ✦

hit the road `about 5 minutes`

Tell your kids, Instead of just talking about remembering, let's remind ourselves of what God has done in our lives and throughout history.

Give each kid a marker and a long strip of paper (from those you cut before the session began) and have them create their own scrolls. Tell them, Like the small mezuzah scrolls that orthodox Jews use to remind them of God, we are going to create a scroll of remembrance—a scroll that contains the things we want to remember about God.

Ask them to spend the next several minutes writing down things that are meaningful for them to remember about God—Scriptures from today, events from the Bible, examples from history, events from their own lives, or truths about God's character.

Allow several minutes for kids to write. Then pass out ribbons/rubber bands for kids to tie up their scrolls. Encourage them to keep their scrolls somewhere they'll see them daily.

Conclude with a very simple prayer: Lord, we love you with all our hearts, souls, and strength. Help us to always remember you in all we say and do. Amen.

Let your kids know you'll be sending **5 for 5 world tour** life application and devotional

playlist

To give ambiance while students create their scrolls, download the song "Never Forget You" by Sonicflood to your iPod (or to a CD) and play it while kids write.

aftr u meet

Right after your meeting, send kids the first **5 for 5 world tour** challenge for them to do tomorrow via Twitter, e-mail, or by posting it on a Facebook page (or youth group Web page) you've set up. Continue to send 1 challenge each day for the 5 days following your meeting.

About 2 days after your group meets, send a text message to your kids, encouraging them to remember what they wrote on their scrolls. Prompt them to keep at it with their **5 for 5 world tour** challenges and let them know you're praying for them.

challenges for them to do each day via Twitter, e-mail, or through a Facebook group you've set up. (Or, if you prefer not to use these technology options, pass out copies of the **5 for 5 world tour** handout you've downloaded from the CD-ROM to the teens.) Encourage your kids to strive to spend about 5 minutes each day connecting with God through these devotional experiences.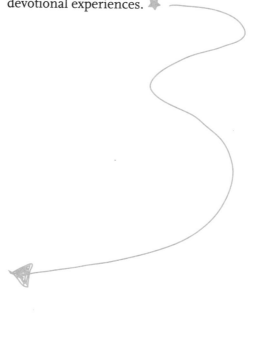

5 for 5 world tour handout

Transforming

The Prep

Session goal: Jr. highers will learn about how Moses' face became radiant after spending time with God; they'll be challenged to consider how God wants to transform their lives through intimacy with him.

Scriptures: Exodus 34:28-35; Isaiah 64:8; Acts 4:13; Romans 12:2; 2 Corinthians 3:18; 1 Timothy 4:7, 8

You'll need:

- Bibles
- Pens or pencils
- Paper
- 2 bags filled with funny clothing and accessories (wigs, scarves, glasses, brushes, makeup, face paint, etc.)
- Several containers of modeling clay or dough (enough for each kid to have 1 piece to mold)
- Glow-in-the-dark stars or other glow objects (1 per teen)
- Several lamps or flashlights

Download and print:

- **solo/strike a chord** discussion guide (1 per teen)
- "Faith Training" handout (1 per teen)

Optional supplies:

- For **backstage pass:** CD player and CD or iPod with recommended **playlist** songs.
- For **hit the road:** Download and print copies of this week's **5 for 5 world tour** take-home page (1 per teen) if you are unable to use the technology options.

Setting it up:

- If you are doing the **mic check** activity, gather some funny clothing, accessories, and makeover supplies. Divide up the items and put them in 2 bags. Then contact 2 people (adult leaders, parents, or kids from the small group who don't mind being a little silly) and ask them to be volunteer models for this activity.
- If you'd like to use the optional **playlist** recommendations, download the songs "Change Me" by Sanctus Real and "New Creation" by Tree63 and ready your iPod or burn a CD in order to play the songs during the session.
- Place your glow-in-the-dark items under the lamps in your meeting area to charge them during the session. If lamps aren't available, collect enough flashlights so kids can charge the items themselves during **backstage pass.**

Leader insight:

Remember the scene from the classic movie *The Ten Commandments* when Moses comes down the mountain after meeting with God? The once young and dapper Charlton Heston appears to have been transformed into an older-looking man with zebra-striped hair who acts a bit zombie-ish!

So the movie took some liberties here, but the reality is that the biblical account is even a bit . . . *weirder*. Exodus 34 records that when Moses came down the mountain, the skin on his face was literally shining. It was so bright—actually radiating light—that he had to wear a veil when he was with other people. (The directors probably figured Charlton Heston in a veil wasn't quite manly enough!) Moses' time in the holy presence of God altered his appearance in a radical and noticeable way.

Paul picks up the imagery of the Exodus account in 2 Corinthians 3 as he compares life under the law with life in the Spirit. As part of his discussion, Paul says that our faces—like Moses'—"reflect the Lord's glory" as we are "being transformed into [Christ's] likeness" (3:18, *NIV*).

At the core of this small group session is *transformation*—the idea that intimacy with God leads to growth and change in our lives. As Moses' appearance was changed after being in God's presence, so should our *lives* be changed from our interactions with God. This process of change is initiated by the Holy Spirit who is powerfully at work in us, producing fruit and transforming our way of thinking.

But the process of change and growth is not all up to God—we shouldn't approach our spiritual lives as if we're on autopilot, sitting passively while we wait for God to do all the work! Spiritual growth and life-change require effort on our part as we seek to know God better through practicing spiritual disciplines like prayer, Bible study, worship, service, fasting, solitude, and others.

Acts 4:13 records that people could tell Peter and John had "been with Jesus" as they observed the radical way their lives had changed. What about you? Can people tell that you've been with Jesus? Does your time with him result in life-change? Does your life glow with godliness? Are you regularly putting in the effort to know God better and grow in intimacy with him? Are you working to strengthen your spiritual muscles as Paul told Timothy: "Train yourself to be godly. 'Physical training is good, but training for godliness is much better, promising benefits in this life and in the life to come'"? (1 Timothy 4:7, 8).

In preparation for leading this small group session, pray: God, I want to experience you as Moses did. I long to be in your presence. I desire to know you more and more. Inspire my jr. highers, Lord, to seek after you with passion. Give them the desire to grow deeper and deeper in intimacy with you. Change me. Form me. Transform me. And help my kids to form a vision for a changed life. Help them to see how you want them to grow, stretch, and change. Plant in them a desire to become more and more Christ-like as they grow in faith. Let our lives shine, Lord, with the light of your love. Amen. ✤

b4 u meet

A couple of days before your group meets, send a text message to your kids reminding them of the upcoming Connect study. (If some teens don't text, send them an e-mail or a message on Facebook or MySpace.)

The Session

Rearrange or delete sections of the study to best meet your group's needs.

txt a frnd [about 5 minutes]

Invite your small group to consider this question:

✳ If you could change one thing about yourself (not a physical trait but rather habits, emotions, mental abilities, etc.), what would it be? Why?

When they've got an answer, invite them to get out their cell phones and text their answer to another person in the room. (If kids don't have their own phone, they could borrow a friend's or could form pairs and talk about their answer to this question.)

When you're ready to move on to the next part of the study, have them put their cell phones away for now. ✳

mic check [about 5 minutes]

Ask your kids if they've ever watched makeover shows. Ask them which is their favorite and why. Then let them know they'll be doing their own makeovers today.

Divide the group into 2 even teams and give each team a bag of supplies. Assign each of the 2 volunteers to 1 of the groups. Then say, Here is what our volunteers look like BEFORE. Now, teams, work together and as fast as you can to see who can come up with the most creative AFTER. You've got 3 minutes to makeover your subjects any way you want. Ready? Go!

Encourage kids to have some good-natured fun as they dress up their volunteer as goofily or differently as possible. Warn teams when they have 1 minute left, and 30 seconds left. Congratulate the kids on their creativity and have the volunteers parade their AFTER looks in front of everyone while the group applauds them.

Say: Today we're going to look at a time when Moses' face got a makeover.

solo [about 5 minutes]

Tell your kids you'd like them to find a spot in your meeting area where they can be alone and spend about 5 minutes reading Scripture and thinking about what it means.

Remind them that last week they read about when the Israelites forgot about God. Now they'll read about the transformation that happened to Moses when he spent time with God.

Give each teen a copy of the **solo/strike a chord** handout and a pen or pencil, inviting them to read and follow the instructions. (Have them read through only the top portion, **solo**, right now, and they'll need the **strike a chord** portion in a few minutes.) Here's a copy of what they'll read:

Take 5 minutes to read Exodus 34:29-35. Consider:

♣ What stands out to you most from this passage? Why?

♣ What do you think went through the Hebrews' minds when they saw Moses glowing?

solo/strike a chord handout

hidden track

In the **Setting it up** section in **The Prep** part of this session, you were encouraged to contact 2 adult or teen volunteers for this activity. Have them be ready now.

When the kids understand what they're supposed to do, have them take off and find a spot to read and reflect. After about 5 minutes, call everybody back together. ✹

solo/strike a chord handout

txt it

If you want, invite kids to answer these questions both by talking aloud and by texting. As some share their answers, others can text them to you. Read some of their thoughts aloud and build upon their ideas as your group explores this topic together.

strike a chord `about 10 to 15 minutes`

ave the group now look at the bottom portion of the **solo/strike a chord** handout, and use it to guide your small group Bible exploration and discussion together as a group. Here's a copy of the **strike a chord** text for you to use to guide your discussion time:

Reread Exodus 34:29-35 together and talk about these questions:

✹ Why do you think Moses wore a veil over his face?

✹ What do you think God's presence must be like if Moses glowed after spending time with him?

✹ What are some ways that people "glow" now after they've spent time with God? (Give examples of ways you can tell that people are close to God.)

Say: Moses had just spent 40 days in God's presence—he had an encounter with God unlike any one else in human history. And that time with God radically changed Moses, inside and out.

Spending time with God—knowing God—changed him. And the same thing changes us.

Look at another example in the Bible. The disciples had been regular guys. John and Peter had been fisherman. Nothing special . . . nothing out of the ordinary. But something changed about them. Invite a volunteer to read aloud Acts 4:13 while everyone else follows along in their own Bibles. Then explain:

✣ The apostles were preaching powerfully, speaking boldly. They were different. They were changed. And everyone knew why: because they'd been with Jesus.

✣ Spending time with Jesus—knowing him—changed Peter and John. And the same thing changes us.

✣ We're changed instantly when we first have faith in Jesus as the Holy Spirit enters our lives. But we're also changed in a gradual, ongoing way. Invite a volunteer to read aloud 2 Corinthians 3:18 while everyone else follows along. Share with your group:

  ● In this passage, Paul is reminding his readers of what happened to Moses—when his face glowed and he wore a veil. Paul is saying that our lives reflect and shine forth God's glory as we become more like God himself.

  ● Pay attention to what he says: Paul writes that God's Spirit "makes us more and more like him." That's not an instant change—that's an ongoing, continuing process. As you spend time with Jesus—daily, hourly, minute-by-minute—you are changed, transformed, completely made over. ✣

freestyle `about 10 minutes`

Think about your own life as a BEFORE and AFTER. What are you like now? How is God at work in your life, changing you to be more like Jesus? In what ways do you want to grow or change more?

Give each teen a piece of modeling clay or dough and have them start squashing it and squeezing it in their hands, to warm it up and make it pliable. As they do, read them the following:

playlist

To add some ambiance to this art experience, download these songs to your iPod (or to a CD) and play them while teens work. Encourage them to listen to the words as well:
"Change Me" by Sanctus Real
"New Creation" by Tree63

Romans 12:2 says, "Don't copy the behavior and customs of this world, but let God transform you into a new person by changing the way you think."

Ask your kids to squeeze their hands into a fist as they hold the clay, then open their fists and look at the shape—the imprint—of their fingers formed onto the clay. This verse points out that we can live our lives as a copy of the world, just as the clay was shaped and conformed to your hand. Or we can allow God to transform us.

Now read Isaiah 64:8: "O LORD, you are our Father. We are the clay, and you are the potter. We all are formed by your hand." Tell your jr. highers: We have a choice: We can conform ourselves to the world, or we can invite God, the potter, to shape us and change us, making us into who he wants us to be.

Now have your group think quietly about the ways they feel God is changing them—or maybe about a way they think God *wants* to change them. Have them take a few minutes to form their clay into a symbol or sculpture that represents that area of change. They don't need to show anybody—just make whatever *they* want. When they're done, they can keep their sculpture and consider it a visual prayer between them and God.

Allow volunteers to share their sculptures if they'd like, but they don't have to. To close this activity, say something like this:

God is changing you—and God wants to change you and grow you even more—but it doesn't just happen on its own. Remember how it happened in Moses' life? It was a direct result of spending time with God—of being close to God. When you are in contact with God—close to him, connected to him, letting him wash over and through your life day after day—he is able to form you and shape you into who he wants you to be. ✦

Faith Training handout

encore   about 10 to 15 minutes

We've explored God's part in our transformation: the work of the Holy Spirit in our lives, purifying us, producing fruit, and transforming us. But we have a part in it, too!

Prompt a volunteer to read aloud 1 Timothy 4:7, 8 while everyone else reads along in their own Bibles. Then say something like this:

Our part is to do the training that's involved in getting to know God better. Just like athletes train, exercising each day, we also need to do spiritual exercises—daily practices and habits that help us grow closer to God and know him better.

Pass out the "Faith Training" handout to everyone. Keep a copy for yourself and briefly talk through the 10 spiritual disciplines highlighted on the page. Add any additional explanations you have that might help your jr. highers understand what these disciplines could look like at their age and in their context.

Then say: One goal I'd like you to have for the next few days is to zero in on one of these faith-training exercises that you feel like you want to focus on in your spiritual life. You may be drawn to focus on one that fits your personality and passions; it may be something you already like to do and that you know helps you feel close to God. Or you may want to try something that's challenging to you. Like athletes who really push themselves to grow stronger through doing tougher exercises, you may choose to try one of these faith-building habits that will be harder for you and may not be a natural fit with your personality.

hidden track

In the **Setting it up** section in **The Prep** part of this session, you were encouraged to place the glow-in-the-dark stars (or other glow objects) under lamps during this session to get them charged up. If you don't have lamps available, pass out some flashlights now so your kids can shine some rays on the items to charge them.

5 for 5 world tour handout

Have kids form pairs or trios and talk about these questions together:

- Which of these spiritual exercises do Christians most often focus on or talk about?
- Which of these spiritual exercises do Christians sometimes overlook or forget about? Why?
- Which of these spiritual exercises seems easiest or most natural to you?
- Which one do you think would be the toughest for you to do?
- Which one do you think God might want you to focus on as you strive to know him better and be changed by him? Why?

backstage pass & hit the road `about 5 minutes`

Point out the lamps in the room and invite kids to pick up a glow-in-the-dark object that has been soaking up the rays. Now turn off the other lights in the room.

Then say: When Moses spent time in God's presence, he became radiant—his face glowed! As you spend time growing closer to God, you too will become radiant—your life will glow and shine for all to see.

Tell kids to take a few minutes to hold their stars in the darkness and pray to God about how they desire to glow in this world because of their closeness to him. Ask them to consider what God wants to do to continue to transform them into his image.

After some time, wrap up with your own prayer aloud.

Let your kids know you'll be sending **5 for 5 world tour** life application and devotional challenges for them to do each day via Twitter, e-mail, or through a Facebook group you've set up. (Or, if you prefer not to use these technology options, pass out copies of the **5 for 5 world tour** handout you've downloaded from the CD-ROM to the teens.) Encourage your kids to strive to spend about 5 minutes each day connecting with God through these devotional experiences. ✦

Right after your meeting, send kids the first **5 for 5 world tour** challenge for them to do tomorrow via Twitter, e-mail, or by posting it on a Facebook page (or youth group Web page) you've set up. Continue to send 1 challenge each day for the 5 days following your meeting.

About 2 days after your group meets, send a text message to your kids, encouraging them to continue to do their spiritual disciplines and connect with God so that he can transform their lives, even now after this small group study is over. Prompt them to keep at it with their final **5 for 5 world tour** challenges and let them know you're praying for them.

Scripture index

You think jr. highers rock,

and you're pumped about relating to them through small groups. We get that. So we created this study with your students in mind.

Crank up the volume with this 9-week small group collision that dives into the **life of Moses**. The sessions dig into Exodus and propel your students to live out their faith in God daily.

inside:

- ✶ media options that utilize texting, music, social networks, and more before, during, and after each study
- ✶ components you can arrange or drop to best meet the needs of your group's age, maturity, and attention span
- ✶ time built in to read each study's Scripture so there's no homework for your students
- ✶ student sheets you can print from the enclosed CD-ROM

This is **A Rock Your Face Off Jr. High Resource,** designed to give you the strategies, tips, and encouragement you need to strike a chord with your students!

CD-ROM
INSIDE!

Y0-DAO-376

RELIGION / Christian Ministry

ISBN 978-0-7847-2405-7

9 780784 72

021532810

Standard®
P U B L I S H I N G

www.standardpub.com

ciy
**CHRIST
IN YOUTH**
RESOURCES